D1077387

ARNOLD

A member of the Hodder Headline Group
LONDON • AUCKLAND

English Grammar for Students of Languages Series
Edited by Jacqueline Morton

First published in the United States of America by
The Olivia and Hill Press

First published in Great Britain in 1999 by
Arnold, a member of the Hodder Headline Group,
338 Euston Road, London NW1 3BH

http://www.arnoldpublishers.com

British Library Cataloguing in Publication Data
A catalogue record for this book is available from the British Library

ISBN 0 340 74198 8

1 2 3 4 5 6 7 8 9 10

Printed and bound in the United States of America

What do you think about this book? Or any other Arnold title?
Please send your comments to feedback.arnold@hodder.co.uk

CONTENTS

CONTENTS

TO THE STUDENT

English Grammar for Students of Spanish explains the grammatical terms that are in your Spanish textbook and shows you how they relate to English grammar. Once you understand the terms and concepts in your own language, it will be easier for you to understand what is being introduced in Spanish. This handbook also points out the similarities and differences between English and Spanish grammar and alerts you to common pitfalls.

Many teachers incorporate *English Grammar* into the class syllabus so their students will know which pages to read before doing an assignment in their Spanish textbook. If you are selecting the pages yourself, check the detailed index at the end of this handbook for the terms and concepts you will need to understand for your textbook assignment. When you finish a chapter in *English Grammar*, you can test your comprehension by doing the short *Reviews* and checking your answers against the *Answer Key* (see p. 183).

———— TIPS FOR STUDYING A FOREIGN LANGUAGE ————

It is generally accepted that the two most important elements in learning a foreign language are vocabulary and grammar. Words (vocabulary) and the way in which they are formed and combined together (grammar) make up the ideas or messages that people wish to communicate. As a student you must learn the vocabulary and grammar presented in the classroom and textbook. This will in turn allow you to develop the four skills of language: listening, speaking, reading, and writing.

The following suggestions will help you improve your ability to learn the vocabulary and grammar and to become a successful foreign language learner.

1. PRACTICE IN SEQUENCE — Your Spanish textbook presents material in a sequential fashion; that is, each chapter and each section of a chapter present new material that depends upon previously learned material. You need to learn the material in the order that it is presented; make sure you understand each section before moving on to the next one. Remember that language learning is like building a house; each brick is only as secure as its foundation.

2. **PRACTICE DAILY** — Set aside a block of time each day for studying Spanish. Don't get behind. It's almost impossible to catch up because you need time to absorb the material and to develop the skills.

3. **LEARN NEW VOCABULARY** — Memorization plays an important role in language learning. For instance, you will have to memorize the new vocabulary items in order to produce them as you speak or write. One way to learn the new vocabulary is by making flashcards. Write each new vocabulary item on a separate index card with Spanish on one side and English on the other. To review, look at the English word. Say the corresponding Spanish word aloud or write it down; then flip the card over to check your answer. You can also use the vocabulary lists in your Spanish textbook to learn new words. First, look at the Spanish words and try to say the corresponding English words. Then look at the English words and try to say or write the corresponding Spanish words.

4. **LEARN NEW GRAMMAR FORMS** — In addition to memorizing vocabulary, you will need to memorize verb conjugations, noun and adjective endings, and other grammatical forms. However, simply memorizing new grammatical forms is not enough. You will need to understand when and how to use the grammatical forms so that you can produce them as you speak or write. By using *English Grammar for Students of Spanish* to compare the grammar structures in English and Spanish, you will learn how these structures function. Once you understand how the grammatical structures function, it will be easier for you to learn to produce the forms by completing the exercises and activities in your Spanish textbook.

5. **LEARN TO COMMUNICATE** — The principle goal of your Spanish instruction is for you to be able to communicate with Spanish speakers and to function in a Spanish-speaking country. Learning vocabulary and grammar is not the end goal; it is a means to develop your ability to communicate. Keeping the goal in mind will help you see the purpose behind the exercises you do and will ultimately help make you a successful language learner.

Buena suerte,

Emily Spinelli

INTRODUCTION

When you learn a foreign language, in this case Spanish, you must look at each word in three ways: MEANING, PART OF SPEECH, and FUNCTION.

MEANING

An English word may be matched with a Spanish word that has a similar meaning.

> *House,* a building in which people live, has the same meaning as the Spanish word **casa.**

Words with equivalent meanings are learned by memorizing vocabulary. Sometimes two words are the same or very similar in both English and Spanish. These words are called COGNATES and are, of course, easy to learn.

SPANISH	ENGLISH
inteligente	intelligent
problema	problem
visitar	visit

Occasionally knowing one Spanish word will help you learn another.

> Knowing that **niño** means *boy* should help you learn that **niña** is *girl;* or knowing that **hermano** is *brother* should help you remember that **hermana** is *sister.*

Usually, however, there is little similarity between words and knowing one Spanish word will not help you learn another. As a general rule, you must memorize each vocabulary item separately.

> Knowing that **hombre** is *man* will not help you learn that **mujer** is *woman.*

In addition, every language has its own phrases or way of expressing ideas; these are called IDIOMATIC EXPRESSIONS, or IDIOMS. For example, *"to fall* asleep" or *"to take* a walk" do not have their usual meaning as in *"to fall* down the stairs," or *"to take* a book to school." You will have to be on the alert for these idioms because they cannot be translated word-for-word in Spanish.

The Spanish equivalent of the English idiom "to fall asleep" is "dormirse" [literally, *"to put oneself to sleep"*] and "to take a walk" is equivalent to the Spanish idiom "**dar** un paseo" [literally, *"to give* a walk"].

PART OF SPEECH

In English and Spanish a word can be classified as belonging to one of eight categories called PARTS OF SPEECH:

adjective	adverb
article	conjunction
noun	preposition
pronoun	verb

Some parts of speech are further broken down according to type. Adjectives, for instance, can be descriptive, interrogative, demonstrative, or possessive. Each part of speech has its own rules for spelling, pronunciation and use.

In order to choose the correct Spanish equivalent of an English word, you will have to identify its part of speech. For example, look at the word *what* in the following sentences.

What do you want?
　　|
interrogative pronoun → **qué**

What movie did you see?
　　|
interrogative adjective → **cuál**

I'll do *what* you want.
　　|
relative pronoun → **lo que**

The English word is the same in all three sentences. In Spanish, however, three different words are used because each *what* belongs to a different part of speech.

FUNCTION

In English and Spanish the role a word plays in a sentence is called its FUNCTION. Depending on the sentence, the same word can have a variety of functions:

subject
direct object
indirect object
object of a preposition

Let us look at the function of the word *him* in the following sentences and see the various functions it can have in a sentence.

They don't see *him*.

direct object → **lo**

I wrote *him* a letter.

indirect object → **le**

Are you going with *him*?

object of a preposition → **él**

The English word is the same in all three sentences, but in Spanish three different words will be used because each *him* has a different function.

In order to choose the correct Spanish equivalent of an English word, you will have to identify its function.

—————————— **SUMMARY** ——————————

As a student of Spanish you must learn to recognize both the part of speech and the function of each word in a sentence. This is essential because words in a Spanish sentence have a great deal of influence on one another.

*My older **brother** works in that large modern **office**.*

Mi **hermano** mayor trabaja en esa **oficina** grande y moderna.

In English, the only word that affects another word in the sentence is *brother*, which forces us to say *works*. If the word were *brothers*, we would have to say *work*.

In Spanish, the word for *brother* (**hermano**) not only affects the word for *works*, (**trabaja**), but also the spelling and pronunciation of the Spanish words for *my* (**mi**) and *older* (**mayor**). The word for *office* (**oficina**) affects the spelling and pronunciation of the Spanish words for *that* (**esa**), *large* (**grande**), and *modern* (**moderna**).

Since parts of speech and function are usually determined in the same way in English and in Spanish, this handbook will show you how to identify them in English. You will then learn to compare English and Spanish constructions, focusing on similarities and differences. This will give you a better understanding of the explanations in your Spanish textbook.

CHAPTER

1

WHAT IS A NOUN?

A **NOUN** is a word that can be the name of
a person, animal, place, thing, event, or idea.

- a person   professor, clown, student, girl, baby
               Professor Smith, Dr. Anderson, Bill, Mary
- an animal   elephant, horse, snake, eagle
                Lassie, Bambi, Garfield, Teddy
- a place   stadium, restaurant, city, state, country
                Madrid, Michigan, Mexico, South America
- a thing   apple, lamp, dress, airplane
                Coca-Cola, the White House, a Cadillac
- an event   graduation, marriage, birth, Thanksgiving
  or activity   the Olympics, shopping, rest, growth
- an idea   democracy, humor, hatred, honor
  or concept   time, love, justice, jealousy, poverty

As you can see, a noun is not only a word that names
something that is tangible (i.e., something you can
touch), such as *lamp, horse,* or *White House,* it can also be
the name of things that are abstract (i.e., that you cannot
touch), such as *justice, jealousy,* and *honor.*

A noun that does not state the name of specific person,
place, or thing, etc. is called a **COMMON NOUN**. A common
noun does not begin with a capital letter, unless it is the
first word of a sentence. All the nouns above that are not
capitalized are common nouns.

A noun that is the name of a specific person, place,
thing, etc. is called a **PROPER NOUN**. A proper noun always
begins with a capital letter. All the nouns above that are
capitalized are proper nouns.

Bill is my friend.

proper   common
noun   noun

A noun that is made up of two or more words is called a
COMPOUND NOUN. A compound noun can be composed of
two common nouns such as *ice cream* or *comic strip,* or two
proper nouns, such as *South America* or *Mexico City.*

IN ENGLISH ───────────────────────────────

To help you learn to recognize nouns, look at the paragraph below where the nouns are in italics.

The *countries* that make up the Spanish-speaking *world* export *products* that we use every *day. Spain* produces many of the *shoes, purses,* and *gloves* that are sold in *stores* throughout the *United States. Spain* also sells us much *wine, sherry,* and *brandy.* The *islands* of the *Caribbean* and the *nations* of *Central America* supply us with tropical *fruits* such as *bananas* and *melons; sugar* is another important *export* of these *regions.* While *oil* is a major *source* of *income* for *Mexico* and *Venezuela,* the *economies* of several other *countries* of *Latin America* depend upon the *production* and *exportation* of *coffee.*

IN SPANISH ───────────────────────────────

Nouns are identified in the same way they are in English.

─────────── TERMS USED TO TALK ABOUT NOUNS ───────────

- GENDER — A noun can have a gender; that is, it can be classified according to whether it is masculine, feminine, or neuter (see *What is Meant by Gender?*, p. 6).
- NUMBER — A noun has number; that is, it can be identified according to whether it is singular or plural (see *What is Meant by Number?*, p. 10).
- FUNCTION —A noun can have a variety of functions in a sentence; that is, it can be the subject of the sentence (see *What is a Subject?*, p. 23) or an object (see *What are Objects?*, p. 124).

— *REVIEW* —

Circle the nouns in the following sentences.

1. Students came into the classroom and spoke to the teacher.

2. The Wilsons went on a tour of Mexico.

3. Figure skating is an exciting event in the Winter Olympics.

4. Buenos Aires, the capital of Argentina, is a cosmopolitan city.

5. Truth is stranger than fiction.

6. They want a boss with intelligence and a sense of humor.

CHAPTER

2

WHAT IS MEANT BY GENDER?

GENDER in the grammatical sense means that a
word can be classified as masculine, feminine, or neuter.

> Did Paul give Mary the book?
> Yes, *he* gave *it* to *her.*
> | | |
>   masc. neuter fem.

GRAMMATICAL GENDER is not very important in English;
however, it is at the very heart of the Spanish language
where the gender of a word is often reflected not only in
the way the word itself is spelled and pronounced, but
also in the way all the words connected to it are spelled
and pronounced.

More parts of speech have a gender in Spanish than in
English.

ENGLISH	SPANISH
pronouns	nouns
possessive adjectives	pronouns
	articles
	adjectives

Since each part of speech follows its own rules to indicate gender, you will find gender discussed in the sections
dealing with articles and the various types of pronouns
and adjectives. In this section we shall only look at the
gender of nouns.

IN ENGLISH

Nouns themselves do not have a gender, but sometimes
their meaning will indicate a gender based on the biological sex of the person or animal the noun stands for. For
example, when we replace a proper or common noun
which refers to a man or a woman, we use *he* for males
and *she* for females.

- nouns referring to males indicate the MASCULINE gender

> Paul came home; *he* was tired; I was glad to see *him.*
> | | |
> noun (male) masculine   masculine

- nouns referring to females indicate the FEMININE gender

> The girl came home; *she* was tired; I was glad to see *her.*
> | | |
> noun (female)   feminine   feminine

All the proper or common nouns that do not have a biological gender are considered NEUTER and are replaced by *it*.

40

The city of Washington is lovely. I enjoyed visiting *it*.
    | |
 noun   neuter

IN SPANISH ────────────────────────────────

All nouns — common nouns and proper nouns — have a gender; they are either masculine or feminine. Do not confuse the grammatical terms "masculine" and "feminine" with the terms "male" and "female." Only a few Spanish nouns have a grammatical gender tied to whether they refer to someone of the male or female sex; most nouns have a gender that must be memorized.

50

The gender of common and proper nouns based on BIOLOGICAL GENDER is easy to determine. These are nouns whose meaning can only refer to one or the other of the biological sexes, male or female.

MALES → MASCULINE	FEMALES → FEMININE
Paul	Mary
boy	girl
brother	sister
stepfather	niece

60

The gender of all other nouns, common and proper, cannot be explained or figured out. These nouns have a GRAMMATICAL GENDER that is unrelated to biological gender and which must be memorized. Here are some examples of English nouns classified under the gender of their Spanish equivalent.

MASCULINE	FEMININE
money	coin
book	library
country	nation
Peru	Argentina
dress	shirt
Wednesday	peace
sorrow	health

70

As you learn a new noun, you should always learn its gender because it will affect the spelling of the words related to it. Textbooks and dictionaries usually indicate the gender of a noun with an *m.* for masculine or an *f.* for feminine. Sometimes the definite articles are used: **el** for masculine or **la** for feminine (see *What are Articles?*, p. 12).

80

──────── Endings indicating gender ────────

Gender can sometimes be determined by looking at the end of the Spanish noun. In the lists that follow there are endings that often indicate feminine nouns and others that indicate masculine nouns. Since you will encounter many nouns with these endings in basic Spanish, it is certainly worthwhile to familiarize yourself with them.[1]

Feminine endings

-a	la casa, la biblioteca	*house, library*
-dad, -tad	la ciudad, la libertad	*city, liberty*
-z	la nariz	*nose*
-ión, -ción	la reunión, la nación	*meeting, nation*
-umbre	la costumbre	*custom*
-ie	la especie	*species*

Masculine endings

Any ending except those provided in the "Feminine endings" list above. In particular:

-l	el papel	*paper*
-o	el libro	*book*
-n	el jardín	*garden*
-e	el parque	*park*
-r	el dolor	*pain*
-s	el interés	*interest*

To help you remember these endings note that for the masculine endings the letters spell "loners."

There are, of course, exceptions to the above rules. For instance, **mano** *(hand)* is a feminine word even though it ends with the letter -o and **día** *(day)* is a masculine word even though it ends with the letter -a. Your textbook and instructor will point out the exceptions that you will need to learn.

CAREFUL — Do not rely on biological gender to indicate the grammatical gender of Spanish equivalents of nouns that can refer to a man or a woman. For instance, the grammatical gender of the noun "**persona**" *(person)* is always feminine, even though the person being referred to could be a man or a woman.

[1]This table of endings has been adapted from John J. Bergen. "A Simplified Approach for Teaching the Gender of Spanish Nouns." *Hispania*, LXI (December, 1978), 875.

— *REVIEW* —

Circle masculine (M) or feminine (F) next to the nouns whose gender you can identify, and (?) next to the nouns whose gender you would have to look up in a dictionary.

GENDER IN SPANISH

1. boys	M	F	?
2. chair	M	F	?
3. Cathy	M	F	?
4. classroom	M	F	?
5. visitor	M	F	?
6. sisters	M	F	?
7. dresses	M	F	?

CHAPTER

3

WHAT IS MEANT BY NUMBER?

1 **NUMBER** in the grammatical sense means that a word can be classified as singular or plural. When a word refers to one person or thing, it is said to be **SINGULAR;** when it refers to more than one, it is **PLURAL.**

one *book*   two *books*
 | |
singular   plural

More parts of speech indicate number in Spanish than in English and there are also more spelling and pronunci-
10 ation changes in Spanish than in English.

ENGLISH	SPANISH
nouns	nouns
verbs	verbs
pronouns	pronouns
demonstrative adjectives	adjectives
	articles

Since each part of speech follows its own rules to indicate number, you will find number discussed in the sections dealing with articles, the various types of adjectives
20 and pronouns, as well as in all the sections on verbs. In this section we shall only look at the number of nouns.

IN ENGLISH ─────────────────────────────

A singular noun is made plural in one of two ways:

1. a singular noun can add an *"-s"* or *"-es"*

book   book*s*
church   church*es*

2. other singular nouns change their spelling

30
man   men
mouse   mice
leaf   leaves
child   children

Some nouns, called **COLLECTIVE NOUNS**, refer to a group of persons or things, but the noun itself is considered singular.

A football *team* has eleven players.
My *family* is well.

IN SPANISH ——————————————————————————

As in English, the plural form of a noun is usually spelled differently from the singular.

1. The most common change is the same as the one made in English; that is, an "-s" is added to singular masculine or feminine nouns that end in a vowel.

	SINGULAR	PLURAL		
MASCULINE	libro	libros	*book*	*books*
FEMININE	mesa	mesas	*table*	*tables*

2. Nouns that end in a consonant add "-es" to form a plural.

	SINGULAR	PLURAL		
MASCULINE	papel	papeles	*paper*	*papers*
FEMININE	ciudad	ciudades	*city*	*cities*

A few nouns will have internal spelling changes when they become plural. Your instructor and textbook will point out the exceptions to the two basic rules listed above.

— REVIEW —

Look at the English and Spanish words below. Indicate if the word is singular (S) or plural (P).

1. teeth   S   P

2. family   S   P

3. dress   S   P

4. mice   S   P

5. coches   S   P

6. mujer   S   P

CHAPTER

4

WHAT ARE ARTICLES?

An ARTICLE is a word placed before a noun to show whether the noun refers to a specific person, animal, place, thing, event, or idea, or whether it refers to an unspecified person, thing, or idea.

I saw *the* boy you spoke about.
a specific boy

I saw *a* boy in the street.
an unspecified boy

In English and in Spanish there are two types of articles, DEFINITE ARTICLES and INDEFINITE ARTICLES.

—————————— **DEFINITE ARTICLES** ——————————

IN ENGLISH

A DEFINITE ARTICLE is used before a noun when we are speaking about a specific person, place, animal, thing, or idea. There is one definite article, *the*.

I read *the* book you recommended.
a specific book

I ate *the* apple you gave me.
a specific apple

The definite article remains *the* even when the noun that follows becomes plural.

I read *the books* you recommended.
I ate *the apples* you gave me.

IN SPANISH

As in English, a definite article is used before a noun when referring to a specific person, place, animal, thing, or idea.

Comí **la** manzana que me diste.
*I ate **the** apple you gave me.*

In Spanish, the definite article is also used when speaking in general terms.

Me gustan **los gatos** pero odio **los perros**.
I like cats [in general] but I hate dogs [in general].

Los perros son más fieles que **los gatos**. 40
Dogs are more faithful than cats.

In Spanish, the article works hand-in-hand with the noun to which it belongs in that it matches the noun's gender and number. This "matching" is called **AGREEMENT**. One says that "the article *agrees* with the noun." (See *What is Meant by Gender?*, p. 6 and *What is Meant by Number?*, p. 10.)

A different article is used, therefore, depending on whether the noun is masculine or feminine (gender) and depending on whether the noun is singular or plural 50 (number).

There are four forms of the definite article: two singular forms and two plural forms.

- **el** indicates that the noun is masculine singular

el libro	*the book*
el muchacho	*the boy*

- **la** indicates that the noun is feminine singular

la casa	*the house*	60
la muchacha	*the girl*

- **los** indicates that the noun is masculine plural

los libros	*the books*
los muchachos	*the boys*

- **las** indicates that the noun is feminine plural

las casas	*the houses*
las muchachas	*the girls*

Memorize nouns with the singular definite article; in most cases the article will tell you if the noun is masculine or 70 feminine.[1]

---

[1]There are only a few exceptions to this statement. The primary exceptions are those feminine nouns that begin with a stressed **a-** and which for pronunciation purposes take **el** as the article: **el agua, el águila**. The noun is nonetheless still feminine: **el agua fría**.

INDEFINITE ARTICLES

IN ENGLISH

An **INDEFINITE ARTICLE** is used before a noun when we are speaking about an unspecified person, animal, place, thing, event, or idea. There are two indefinite articles, *a* and *an*.

- *a* is used before a word beginning with a consonant[1]

  I saw *a* boy in the street.
  |
  not a specific boy

- *an* is used before a word beginning with a vowel

  I ate *an* apple.
  |
  not a specific apple

The indefinite article is used only with a singular noun; it is dropped when the noun becomes plural. At times the word *some* is used to replace it, but it is usually omitted.

  I saw boys in the street.
  I saw *(some)* boys in the street.

  I ate apples.
  I ate *(some)* apples.

IN SPANISH

As in English, an indefinite article is used before a noun when we are not speaking about a specific person, animal, place, thing, event, or idea.

Just as with definite articles, indefinite articles must agree with the noun's gender and number.

There are four forms of the indefinite article: two singular forms and two plural forms.

- **un** indicates that the noun is masculine singular

  | **un** libro | *a book* |
  | **un** muchacho | *a boy* |

- **una** indicates that the noun is feminine singular

  | **una** casa | *a house* |
  | **una** muchacha | *a girl* |

- **unos** indicates that the noun is masculine plural

  | **unos** libros | *(some) books* |
  | **unos** muchachos | *(some) boys* |

---

[1]Vowels are the sounds associated with the letters *a, e, i, o, u* and sometimes *y*; consonants are the sounds associated with the other letters of the alphabet.

- **unas** indicates that the noun is feminine plural

120

unas casas	*(some) houses*
unas muchachas	*(some) girls*

Your textbook will instruct you on additional uses of the definite and indefinite articles in Spanish.

CAREFUL — Unlike English where a noun can be used without an article (*Truth* is stranger than *fiction*; *Mexico* is a beautiful *country*), Spanish common and proper nouns are usually preceded by an article: definite or indefinite.

— REVIEW —

Below is a list of English nouns preceded by a definite or indefinite article.

- Write the Spanish article for each noun on the line provided. The Spanish dictionary entry shows you if the noun (n.) is masculine (m.) or feminine (f.).

	DICTIONARY ENTRY	SPANISH ARTICLE
1. the books	**libro** (n. m.)	_____
2. a table	**mesa** (n. f.)	_____
3. some classes	**clase** (n. f.)	_____
4. the telephone	**teléfono** (n. m.)	_____
5. a car	**coche** (n. m.)	_____
6. the sisters	**hermana** (n. f.)	_____
7. some men	**hombre** (n. m.)	_____
8. an apple	**manzana** (n. f.)	_____
9. the ball	**pelota** (n. f.)	_____

WHAT IS THE POSSESSIVE?

The term **POSSESSIVE** means that one noun owns or *possesses* another noun.

Mary's Spanish book is on the table.
  | |
possessor   possessed

IN ENGLISH ────────────────────────────────

There are two constructions to show possession.

1. An apostrophe can be used. In this construction, the possessor comes before the possessed.

- singular possessor adds an apostrophe + "s"

  Mary's dress
  a tree's branches
  |
  singular possessor

- plural possessor ending with "s" adds an apostrophe after the "s"

  the students' teacher
  the girls' club
  |
  plural possessor

- plural possessor not ending with "s" adds an apostrophe + "s"

  the children's playground
  the men's department
  |
  plural possessor

2. The word *of* can be used. In this structure, the possessed comes before the possessor.

- a singular or plural possessor is preceded by *of the* or *of a*

  the book *of the* professor
  the branches *of a* tree
  |
  singular possessor

  the teacher *of the* students
  |
  plural possessor

IN SPANISH ───────────────────────────────
There is only one way to express possession and that is by using the "of" construction (No. 2). The apostrophe structure (No. 1) does not exist.

The Spanish structure parallels the English structure: the noun possessed + **de** ("of") + definite or indefinite article + the noun possessor. 40

Mary's dress	el vestido **de** María
possessor possessed	possessed possessor
	the dress of Mary
the professor's book	el libro **del** profesor
	de + el
	the book of the professor
the lady's purse	la bolsa **de la** señora	50
	the purse of the lady
a tree's branches	las ramas **de un** árbol
	the branches of a tree
the girls' father	el padre **de las** muchachas
	the father of the girls
the boys' team	el equipo **de los** muchachos
	the team of the boys

— REVIEW —

Below are possessives using the apostrophe. Write the alternate English structure which is the word-for-word equivalent of the Spanish structure.

1. some children's parents

───────────────────────────────

2. the doctor's office

───────────────────────────────

3. a car's speed

───────────────────────────────

4. the girls' soccer coach

───────────────────────────────

5. Gloria Smith's mother

───────────────────────────────

CHAPTER

6

WHAT IS A VERB?

A **VERB** is a word that indicates the action of the sentence.
The word "action" is used in the broadest sense,
not necessarily physical action.

Let us look at different types of words that are verbs:

- a physical activity   to run, to hit, to talk, to walk
- a mental activity   to hope, to believe, to imagine,
                            to dream, to think
- a condition   to be, to have, to seem

Many verbs, however, do not fall neatly into one of the
above three categories. They are verbs nevertheless
because they represent the "action" of the sentence.

The book *costs* only $5.00.
|
to cost

The students *seem* tired.
|
to seem

The verb is the most important word in a sentence. You
cannot write a **COMPLETE SENTENCE**, that is, express a complete thought, without a verb.

It is important to identify verbs because the function of
words in a sentence often depends on the word's relationship to the verb. For instance, the subject of a sentence is
the word doing the action of the verb, and the object is
the word receiving the action of the verb (see *What is a
Subject?*, p. 23, and *What are Objects?*, p. 124).

IN ENGLISH ─────────────────────────────

To help you learn to recognize verbs, look at the paragraph below where the verbs are in italics.

The three students *entered* the restaurant, *selected* a
table, *hung* up their coats and *sat* down. They *looked*
at the menu and *asked* the waitress what she *recommended*. She *advised* the daily special, beef stew. It
was not expensive. They *chose* a bottle of red wine
and *ordered* a salad. The service *was* slow, but the
food *tasted* very good. Good cooking, they *decided*,

takes time. They *ate* pastry for dessert and *finished* the meal with coffee.

IN SPANISH

Verbs are identified the same way that they are in English.   40

TERMS TO TALK ABOUT VERBS

- INFINITIVE OR DICTIONARY FORM — The verb form that is the name of the verb is called an infinitive: *to eat, to sleep, to drink* (see *What is the Infinitive?*, p. 20). In the dictionary a verb is listed without the "to": *eat, sleep, drink*.

- CONJUGATION — A verb is conjugated or changes in form to agree with its subject: *I do, he does* (see *What is a Verb Conjugation?*, p. 35).

- TENSE—A verb indicates tense, that is, the time (present,   50 past, or future) of the action: *I am, I was, I will be* (see *What is Meant by Tense?*, p. 56).

- MOOD — A verb shows mood, that is the speaker's attitude toward what he or she is saying (see *What is Meant by Mood?*, p. 69).

- VOICE — A verb shows voice, that is, the relation between the subject and the action of the verb (see *What is Meant by Active and Passive Voice?*, p. 91).

- PARTICIPLE—A verb may be used to form a participle: *writing, written, singing, sung* (see *What is a Participle?*,   60 p. 63).

- TRANSITIVE OR INTRANSITIVE — A verb can be classified as transitive or intransitive depending on whether or not the verb can take a direct object (see *What are Objects?*, p. 124).

— REVIEW —

Circle the verbs in the following sentences.

1. The students purchase their lunch at school.

2. Paul and Mary were happy.

3. They enjoyed the movie, but they preferred the book.

4. Paul ate dinner, finished his novel, and then went to bed.

5. It was sad to see the little dog struggle to get out of the lake.

6. I attended a concert to celebrate the New Year.

CHAPTER

7

WHAT IS THE INFINITIVE?

The INFINITIVE form is the name of the verb.
The Spanish equivalent of the verb *to study* is **estudiar**.

infinitive

IN ENGLISH

The infinitive is composed of two words: *to* + the DICTIO-NARY FORM of the verb *(to speak, to dance)*. By infinitive we mean the form of the verb that is listed as the entry in the dictionary *(speak, dance)*.

Although the infinitive is the most basic form of the verb, it can never be used in a sentence without another verb which is conjugated (see *What is a Verb Conjugation?*, p. 35).

To learn is exciting.

infinitive conjugated verb

It *is* important *to be* on time.

conjugated verb infinitive

Paul and Mary *want to dance* together.

conjugated verb infinitive

The dictionary form of the verb, rather than the infinitive, is used after such verbs as *let, must, should,* and *can.*

Mr. Smith *let* his daughter *drive* his new car.

dictionary form

Paul *must be* home by noon.

dictionary form

IN SPANISH

The infinitive form is composed of only one word. The word *to* that is part of the English infinitive has no Spanish equivalent. The Spanish infinitive is identified by the last two letters of the verb called THE ENDING.

hablar	*to speak*
comer	*to eat*
vivir	*to live*

The infinitive form is important not only because it is the form under which a verb is listed in the dictionary, but because the ending indicates the pattern the verb will follow to create its various forms.

1ˢᵀ CONJUGATION — verbs ending in -ar follow one pattern
2ᴺᴰ CONJUGATION — verbs ending in -er follow another pattern
3ᴿᴰ CONJUGATION — verbs ending in -ir follow another pattern

In a sentence the infinitive form is always used for a verb that follows any verb other than ser *(to be)*, estar *(to be)*, or **haber** *(to have)*.

John and Mary want to dance together.
Juan y María quieren **bailar** juntos.
                               |
                          infinitive

I can leave tomorrow.
Puedo **salir** mañana.
          |
      infinitive

You should study more.
Usted debe **estudiar** más.
                  |
              infinitive

Notice that in the last two examples there is no "to" in the English sentence to alert you that an infinitive must be used in Spanish.

CAREFUL — You cannot depend upon the English sentence to alert you to the use of the infinitive in Spanish. Often the word "to" will not be used in the English sentence but the infinitive must be used in Spanish.

———————————— CONSULTING THE DICTIONARY ————————————

In English it is possible to change the meaning of a verb by placing short words (prepositions or adverbs) after it.

For example, the verb *look* in Column A below changes meaning depending on the word that follows it *(to, after, for, into)*. In Spanish it is not generally possible to change the meaning of a verb by adding a preposition or an adverb as in Column A. An entirely different Spanish verb corresponds to each meaning.

COLUMN A		MEANING	SPANISH
to look	→	to look at	**mirar**
		I *looked at* the photo.	
to look for	→	to search for	**buscar**
		I *am looking for* my book.	

80

to look after → to take care of **cuidar**
I *am looking after* the children.

to look into → to study **estudiar**
We *'ll look into* the problem.

When consulting an English-Spanish dictionary, all the examples above under Column A can be found under the dictionary entry *look* (**mirar**); however, you will have to search under that entry for the specific expression *look for* (**buscar**) or *look after* (**cuidar**) to find the correct Spanish equivalent.

90

Don't select the first entry under *look* and then add on the Spanish equivalent for *after, for, into*, etc.; the result will be meaningless in Spanish.

— *REVIEW* —

Circle the words that you would replace with an infinitive in Spanish.

1. Mary has nothing more to do today.

2. You must study your lesson.

3. Jeff wants to learn Spanish.

4. They cannot leave on Tuesday.

5. We hope to travel through Spain this summer.

WHAT IS A SUBJECT?

In a sentence the person or thing that performs the action of the verb is called the SUBJECT.   1

To find the subject of a sentence, always look for the verb first; then ask, *who?* or *what?* before the verb (see *What is a Verb?*, p. 18). The answer will be the subject.[1]

> Teresa speaks Spanish.
>> VERB: speaks
>> Who speaks Spanish? ANSWER: Teresa.
>> *Teresa* is the subject.
>> The subject is singular (see p. 10). It refers to one person.   10

> Teresa's books cost a lot of money.
>> VERB: cost
>> What costs a lot of money? ANSWER: books.
>> *Books* is the subject.
>> The subject is plural. It refers to more than one thing.

If a sentence has more than one verb, you have to find the subject of each verb.

> The boys were cooking while Mary set the table.
>> *Boys* is the subject of *were.*
>> (Note that the subject is plural.)   20
>> *Mary* is the subject of *set.*
>> (Note that the subject is singular.)

IN ENGLISH ─────────────────────────────────

Always ask *who?* or *what?* before the verb to find the subject. Never assume that the first word in the sentence is the subject. Subjects can be located in several different places, as you can see in the following examples (the subject is in **boldface** and verb *italicized*):

> *Did* **the game** *start* on time?   30
> After playing for two hours, **Paul** *became* exhausted.
> Mary's **brothers** *arrived* yesterday.

---

[1]The subject performs the action in an active sentence, but is acted upon in a passive sentence (see *What is Meant by Active and Passive Voice?*, p. 91).

IN SPANISH ———————————————————————

The subject of a sentence is identified the same way as it is in English. Also, as in English, it can be located in different places in the sentence.

40

CAREFUL — In both English and Spanish it is important to find the subject of each verb to make sure that the verb form agrees with the subject (see *What is a Verb Conjugation?*, p. 35).

— *REVIEW* —

Find the subjects in the sentences below.
- Next to Q, write the question you need to ask to find the subject of the sentences below.
- Next to A, write the answer to the question you just asked.
- Circle if the subject is singular (S) or plural (P).

1. When the bell rang, all the children ran out.

Q: _____

A: _____   S   P

Q: _____

A: _____   S   P

2. One waiter took the order and another brought the food.

Q: _____

A: _____   S   P

Q: _____

A: _____   S   P

3. The first-year students voted for the class president.

Q: _____

A: _____   S   P

4. They say that Spanish is a beautiful language.

Q: _____

A: _____   S   P

Q: _____

A: _____   S   P

WHAT IS A PRONOUN?

A **PRONOUN** is a word used in place of one or more nouns. It may stand, therefore, for a person, animal, place, thing, event, or idea.

For instance, rather than repeating the proper noun "Paul" in the following sentences, "Paul" can be replaced by a pronoun in the second sentence.

Paul likes to swim. Paul practices every day.
Paul likes to swim. *He* practices every day.

A pronoun can only be used to refer to someone (or something) that has already been mentioned. The word that the pronoun replaces or refers to is called the **ANTECEDENT** of the pronoun. In the example above, the pronoun *he* refers to the proper noun *Paul. Paul* is the antecedent of the pronoun *he.*

There are different types of pronouns, each serving a different function and following different rules. Listed below are the more important types and the chapters in which they are discussed.

PERSONAL PRONOUNS — These pronouns replace nouns referring to persons or things that have been previously mentioned. A different set of pronouns is often used depending on the pronoun's function in the sentence.

- subject (see p. 23)

    I go; *they* read; *he* runs; *she* sings.

- direct object pronouns (see p. 131)

    John loves *her.* Jane saw *him* at the theater.

- indirect object pronouns (see p. 131)

    John gave *us* the book. My mother wrote *me* a letter.

- object of preposition pronouns (p. 139)

    Robert is going to the movies with *us.*
    Don't step in the puddle; walk around *it.*

REFLEXIVE PRONOUNS — These pronouns refer back to the subject of the sentence (see p. 143).

    I cut *myself.* We washed *ourselves.* Mary dressed *herself.*

INTERROGATIVE PRONOUNS — These pronouns are used to ask questions (see p. 153).

Who is that? *What* do you want?

DEMONSTRATIVE PRONOUNS — These pronouns are used to point out persons or things (see p. 161).

This (one) is expensive. *That (one)* is cheap.

POSSESSIVE PRONOUNS — These pronouns are used to show possession or ownership (see p. 148).

Whose book is that? *Mine. Yours* is on the table.

RELATIVE PRONOUNS — These pronouns are used to introduce relative subordinate clauses (see p. 167).

The man *who* is my instructor is very nice.
This is the sweater *that* I bought last week.

INDEFINITE PRONOUNS — These pronouns are used to refer to unidentified persons or things (see p. 178).

One doesn't do that.
Something is wrong.

Spanish indefinite pronouns correspond in usage to their English equivalents. They can be studied in your textbook.

IN ENGLISH ───────────────────────────

Each type of pronoun follows a different set of rules.

IN SPANISH ───────────────────────────

As in English, each type of pronoun follows a different set of rules. Moreover, Spanish pronouns usually correspond in gender and number with their antecedent.

— REVIEW —

Circle the pronouns in the sentences below.
- Draw an arrow from the pronoun to its antecedent, or antecedents if there is more than one.

1. Did Mary call Peter? Yes, she called him last night.

2. That coat and dress are elegant but they are expensive.

3. Isabel baked the cookies herself.

4. Robert and I are very tired. We went out last night.

5. Since the book is not on the desk, it might be inside.

WHAT IS A SUBJECT PRONOUN?

A **SUBJECT PRONOUN** is a pronoun used
as a subject of a verb.

1

> *He* worked while *she* read.
> Who worked? ANSWER: He.
> *He* is the subject of the verb *worked*.
>
> Who read? ANSWER: She.
> *She* is the subject of the verb *read*.

Subject pronouns are divided into three groups: 1ˢᵗ, 2ⁿᵈ,
and 3ʳᵈ person pronouns. The word **PERSON** in this instance
does not necessarily mean a human being. It is a grammatical term.

10

IN ENGLISH

Here is a list of subject pronouns.

1ˢᵀ PERSON

I → the person speaking → SINGULAR

we → the person speaking plus others → PLURAL

> *Mary and I* are free this evening. *We* are going out.

2ⁿᴰ PERSON

you → the person or persons spoken to → SINGULAR or PLURAL

20

> *Paul*, do *you* sing folksongs?
> *Peter, Paul and Mary*, do *you* sing folksongs?

3ᴿᴰ PERSON

he, she, it → the person or object spoken about → SINGULAR

they → the persons or objects spoken about → PLURAL

> *Mary and Paul* are free this evening. *They* are going out.

IN SPANISH

Spanish subject pronouns are also identified as 1ˢᵗ, 2ⁿᵈ and
3ʳᵈ persons, each having a singular and a plural form.
There are three English subject pronouns that have more
than one equivalent in Spanish: *you, we,* and *they.* Also
there is one English subject pronoun, *it,* that has no
equivalent in Spanish because it is generally not
expressed.

30

Subject pronouns are usually presented in the following
order:

SINGULAR		
1ST PERSON	I	yo
2ND PERSON	you	tú
3RD PERSON	he	él
	she	ella
	you	usted

PLURAL		
1ST PERSON	we	nosotros
		nosotras
2ND PERSON	you	vosotros
		vosotras
3RD PERSON	they	ellos
		ellas
	you	ustedes

Although "you" is a 2ⁿᵈ person pronoun since "you" is the person spoken to, two of its forms, **usted** and **ustedes**, are listed with 3ʳᵈ person pronouns because they use the same forms as 3ʳᵈ person pronouns.

Let us look at the English subject pronouns that are either not expressed in Spanish *(it)*, or that have more than one Spanish equivalent *(you, we* and *they)*.

─────────── **"YOU"** (2ⁿᵈ person singular and plural) ───────────

IN ENGLISH

The same pronoun "you" is used to address one or more than one person.

> Mary, are *you* coming with me?
> Mary and Paul, are *you* coming with me?

The same pronoun "you" is used to address the President of the United States or your dog.

> Do *you* have any questions, Mr. President?
> *You* are a good dog, Heidi.

IN SPANISH

There are several words for "you" in Spanish. **Tú**, **vosotros** and **vosotras** are called FAMILIAR "YOU." **Usted** and **ustedes** are called FORMAL "YOU."

─────────── FAMILIAR "YOU" → TÚ, VOSOTROS OR VOSOTRAS ───────────

The familiar forms of "you" are used to address members of one's family (notice that the word "familiar" is similar to the word "family"), persons you call by their first name, children, and pets.

1. to address one person → **tú** (2ⁿᵈ person singular)

Mary, how are you?
|
tú

80

John, how are you?
|
tú

2. to address more than one person → **vosotros** or **vosotras** (2ⁿᵈ person plural)

- to address a group of two or more males → **vosotros**

John and Paul, how are you?
|————┬————| |
masc. pl.   **vosotros** (masc. pl.)

90

- to address a group of two or more females → **vosotras**

Mary and Gloria, how are you?
|————┬————| |
fem. pl.   **vosotras** (fem. pl.)

- to address a group of males and females → **vosotros**

John, Gloria and Mary, how are you?
| | | |
masc.   fem.   fem.   **vosotros** (masc. pl.)

The familiar plural forms **vosotros** and **vosotras** are used only in Spain. In Latin America **ustedes** is used as the plural of **tú** (see below).

100

──────── **FORMAL "YOU"** → USTED AND USTEDES ────────

The formal forms of "you" are used to address persons you do not know well enough to call by a first name or to whom you should show respect (Ms. Smith, Mr. Jones, Dr. Anderson, Professor Gómez).

1. to address one person → **usted** (singular)

Mr. García, how are you?
|
usted

110

Mrs. García, how are you?
|
usted

2. to address a group of males or females → **ustedes** (plural)

Profesor Gómez and Mrs. García, how are you?
| | |
masc. sing.   fem. sing.   **ustedes**

In Latin America **ustedes** is the plural of both the familiar and formal forms.

120

CAREFUL — If in doubt as to whether to use the familiar or formal forms when addressing an adult, use the formal forms. They show respect for the person you are talking to and use of familiar forms might be considered rude.

─────────── CHOOSING THE PROPER FORM OF "YOU" ───────────

In order to choose the correct form of *you* in Spanish, you should go through the following steps:

1. Determine whether the familiar or formal form is appropriate.
2. If the familiar form is appropriate, determine how many persons are being addressed:
   A. one person → **tú**
   B. more than one person:
   ▪ IN LATIN AMERICA → **ustedes**
   ▪ IN SPAIN → determine the sex of the persons being addressed:
   a) a group of males or males and females → **vosotros**
   b) a group of females → **vosotras**
3. If the formal form is appropriate, determine how many persons are being addressed:
   A. one person → **usted**
   B. more than one person → **ustedes**

Here is a chart you can use as a reference.

		ENGLISH	SPANISH	LATIN AMERICA
			SPAIN	
FAMILIAR	SINGULAR	*you*	tú	tú
	PLURAL	*you*	vosotros vosotras	ustedes
FORMAL	SINGULAR	*you*	usted	usted
	PLURAL	*you*	ustedes	ustedes

Let's find the Spanish equivalent for *you* in the following sentences:

John, are you coming with us?
  FAMILIAR OR FORMAL: familiar
  SINGULAR OR PLURAL: singular
  SELECTION: **tú**
Juan, ¿vienes **tú** con nosotros?

Isabel and Gloria, are you coming with us?
FAMILIAR OR FORMAL: familiar
SINGULAR OR PLURAL: plural
SPAIN OR LATIN AMERICA: Spain
MALES, FEMALES OR MIXED GROUP: females
SELECTION: **vosotras**
Isabel y Gloria, ¿venís **vosotras** con nosotros? 170

Vincent and John, are you coming with us?
FAMILIAR OR FORMAL: familiar
SINGULAR OR PLURAL: plural
SPAIN OR LATIN AMERICA: Latin America
SELECTION: **ustedes**
Vicente y Juan, ¿vienen **ustedes** con nosotros?

Mr. President, are you coming with us?
FAMILIAR OR FORMAL: formal
SINGULAR OR PLURAL: singular 180
SELECTION: **usted**
Señor Presidente, ¿viene **usted** con nosotros?

Mr. and Mrs. Lado, are you coming with us?
FAMILIAR OR FORMAL: formal
SINGULAR OR PLURAL: plural
SELECTION: **ustedes**
Señor y señora Lado, ¿vienen **ustedes** con nosotros?

"IT" (3ʳᵈ person singular)

IN ENGLISH 190

Whenever you are speaking about one thing or idea, you use the subject pronoun *it*.

> Where is the book? *It* is on the table.
> John has an idea. *It* is very interesting.

IN SPANISH

The subject pronoun *it* is not generally expressed.

> ¿Dónde está el libro? **Está** sobre la mesa.
> *It* is understood as part of the verb está.
> *Where is the book? It is on the table.* 200

"WE" (1ˢᵗ person plural)

IN ENGLISH

The subject pronoun *we* refers to the person speaking plus others.

> *John and I* are going to the movies.
> *We* are leaving at 7:00.

IN SPANISH

The subject pronoun used depends on the gender of the noun *we* replaces; i.e., the Spanish pronoun must agree with the gender of the antecedent.

- masculine antecedents → **nosotros**

    Juan y yo vamos al cine. **Nosotros** salimos a las 7.
    　　|　　　|　　　　　　　　　　　|
    masc.　masc.　　　　　　　masc. pl.
    antecedents　　　　　　　pronoun
    John and I are going to the movies. We are leaving at 7:00.

- feminine antecedent → **nosotras**

    María y yo vamos al cine. **Nosotras** salimos a las 7.
    　　|　　|　　　　　　　　　　　|
    fem.　fem.　　　　　　　　fem. pl.
    antecedents　　　　　　　pronoun
    Mary and I are going to the movies. We are leaving at 7:00.

- antecedents of different genders → **nosotros**

    Juan, María y yo vamos al cine. **Nosotros** salimos a las 7.
    　|　　　|　　　|　　　　　　　　　　|
    masc. fem.　masc. or fem.　　masc. pl.
    └── antecedents ┘　　　　pronoun
    John, Mary and I are going to the movies. We are leaving at 7:00.

─────────── **"THEY"** (3ʳᵈ **person plural**) ───────────

IN ENGLISH

Whenever you are speaking about more than one person or object, you use the subject pronoun *they.*

> My brothers play tennis. *They* practice a lot.
> My sisters play soccer. *They* practice every day.
> Where are the books? *They* are on the table.

IN SPANISH

The subject pronoun used depends on the gender of the noun it replaces; i.e., the Spanish pronoun must agree with the gender of the antecedent.

- masculine antecedent → **ellos**

    Mis hermanos juegan al tenis. **Ellos** practican todos los días.
    　　　|　　　　　　　　　　　　|
    masc. pl.　　　　　　　masc. pl.
    antecedent　　　　　　pronoun
    My brothers play tennis. They practice every day.

- feminine antecedent → **ellas**

Mis hermanas juegan al fútbol. **Ellas** practican todos los días.
    | |
fem. pl.   fem. pl.
antecedent   pronoun
*My sisters play soccer. **They** practice every day.*

250

- antecedents of different genders → **ellos**

Juan, María y Gloria juegan al fútbol. **Ellos** practican todos los días.
  | | | |
masc. fem. fem.   masc. pl.
 ⌞ antecedents ⌟   pronoun
*John, Mary and Gloria play soccer. **They** practice every day.*

Just as the subject pronoun *it* is not expressed in Spanish, the subject pronoun *they* is not expressed when *they* refers to something other than people.

260

¿Dónde están los libros? **Están** sobre la mesa.
They is understood as part of the verb **están**.
*Where are the books? **They are** on the table.*

— *REVIEW* —

A. Write the corresponding person and number for the words in italics.

■ Write the Spanish subject pronoun that you would use to replace the words in italics. If no pronoun is needed, write "0" in the space under Spanish subject pronoun.

	PERSON	NUMBER	SPANISH SUBJECT PRONOUN
1. *I* am very tired.	_____	_____	_____
2. *It* is very hot outside.	_____	_____	_____
3. *Mary and I* are leaving today.	_____	_____	_____
4. My keys? I think *they* are on the table.	_____	_____	_____
5. "Where do your parents live?" "*They* live in New Jersey."	_____	_____	_____
6. *Gloria and Anita* are my best friends.	_____	_____	_____

B. Write the form of "you" that would be used in each instance.

	SPAIN	LATIN AMERICA
1. Mr. and Mrs. Fuentes, how are *you?*	_____	_____
2. Teresa, where are *you* going?	_____	_____
3. Señorita Acosta, will *you* please finish this report?	_____	_____
4. Come on children, *you* must go to bed.	_____	_____
5. Daddy, will *you* play a game with me?	_____	_____
6. Professor Suárez, *you* haven't given us our homework for tomorrow.	_____	_____

11

WHAT IS A VERB CONJUGATION?

A VERB CONJUGATION is a list of the six possible forms of the
verb for a particular tense. For each tense, there is
one verb form for each of the six persons
used as the subject of the verb.

1

> I am
> you are
> he, she, it is
> we are
> you are
> they are

10

Different tenses have different verb forms, but the principle of conjugation remains the same. In this chapter all
our examples are in the present tense.

IN ENGLISH

The verb *to be* conjugated above is the English verb that
changes the most; it has three forms: *am, are,* and *is.* (In
conversation the initial vowel is often replaced by an
apostrophe: *I'm, you're, he's.*) Other English verbs only
have two forms. Let us look at the verb *to sing.*

SINGULAR		
1ST PERSON	I *sing*	
2ND PERSON	you *sing*	
3RD PERSON	he *sings*	
	she *sings*	
	it *sings*	
PLURAL		
1ST PERSON	we *sing*	
2ND PERSON	you *sing*	
3RD PERSON	they *sing*	

20

Because English verbs change so little, it isn't necessary
to learn "to conjugate a verb"; that is, to list all its possible
forms. For most verbs, it is much simpler to say that the
verb adds an "-s" in the 3rd person singular.

30

IN SPANISH

Unlike English, Spanish verb forms change from one person to another so that when you learn a new verb, you
must also learn how to conjugate it. First, you must establish whether the verb is regular or irregular.

- Verbs whose forms follow a predictable pattern are called REGULAR VERBS. Only one example must be memorized and the pattern can then be applied to other verbs in the same group.
- Verbs whose forms do not follow a predictable pattern are called IRREGULAR VERBS. The conjugation of these verbs must be memorized individually.

───── CHOOSING THE PROPER "PERSON" (see p. 27) ─────

Below is the conjugation of the regular verb **cantar** *(to sing)*. Notice that each of the six persons has its own ending and that different pronouns belonging to the same person have the same verb form. Since the subject pronouns **usted** and **ustedes** use the verb form of the 3ʳᵈ person, they are listed with that person. Therefore, él, **ella** and **usted**, have the same verb form: **canta**.

SINGULAR		
1ˢᵀ PERSON	yo canto	*I sing*
2ᴺᴰ PERSON	tú cantas	*you sing*
3ᴿᴰ PERSON	él canta	*he sings, it sings*
	ella canta	*she sings, it sings*
	usted canta	*you sing*
PLURAL		
1ˢᵀ PERSON	nosotros cantamos	*we sing*[1]
	nosotras cantamos	*we sing*
2ᴺᴰ PERSON	vosotros cantáis	*you sing*
	vosotras cantáis	*you sing*
3ᴿᴰ PERSON	ellos cantan	*they sing*
	ellas cantan	*they sing*
	ustedes cantan	*you sing*

To choose the proper verb form, it is important to identify the person (1ˢᵗ, 2ⁿᵈ or 3ʳᵈ) and the number (singular or plural) of the subject.

1ˢᵀ PERSON SINGULAR — The subject is always **yo** *(I)*.

> Generalmente **yo canto** bien.
> *Generally I sing well.*

Notice that **yo** is not capitalized except when it is the first word of a sentence.

---

[1]Many textbooks only list **nosotros** and **vosotros**. The same verb form applies to **nosotras** and **vosotras**.

2ᴺᴰ PERSON SINGULAR — The subject is always **tú** *(you)*.
> Juan, **tú cantas** muy bien.
> *John, you sing very well.*

3ᴿᴰ PERSON SINGULAR — The subject can be expressed in one of four ways:

1. the 3ʳᵈ person singular masculine pronoun **él** *(he)* and the 3ʳᵈ person singular feminine pronoun **ella** *(she)*   90
> Generalmente **él canta** muy bien.
> *Generally he sings very well.*
>
> Generalmente **ella canta** muy bien.
> *Generally she sings very well.*

2. the singular pronoun **usted** *(you)*
> Señor Gómez, **usted canta** muy bien.
> *Mr. Gómez, you sing very well.*
>
> Señorita Gómez, **usted canta** muy bien.
> *Miss Gómez, you sing very well.*   100

The pronoun **usted** is generally abbreviated as **Ud.** The abbreviation is used far more frequently than the entire word.

3. a proper noun
> María **canta** muy bien.
> *Mary sings very well.*
>
> Pedro **canta** muy bien.
> *Peter sings very well.*
>
> El señor García **canta** muy bien.
> *Mr. Garcia sings very well.*   110

In these three sentences the proper noun could be replaced by the pronoun *she* (**ella** fem.) or *he* (**él** masc.) so that you must use the 3ʳᵈ person singular form of the verb.

4. a singular common noun
> El hombre **canta** muy bien.
> *The man sings very well.*
>
> La niña **canta** muy bien.
> *The girl sings very well.*   120

In these two sentences the common noun could be replaced by the pronoun *she* (**ella** fem.) or *he* (**él** masc.) so that you must use the 3ʳᵈ person singular form of the verb.

Remember that the subject pronoun *it* has no Spanish equivalent. *It* as a subject is generally not expressed but rather understood as part of the verb. (See *What is a Subject Pronoun?*, p. 27.)

> Juan y María tienen un párajo. **Canta** muy bien.
> *John and Mary have a bird. It sings very well.*

130

1ˢᵀ PERSON PLURAL — The subject can be expressed in one of two ways:

1. the first person plural pronoun **nosotros** or **nosotras** *(we)*

> Nosotros **cantamos** bien.
> *We sing well.*

2. a multiple subject in which the speaker is included

> Miguel, Gloria y yo **cantamos** muy bien.
> └────┬────┘
>   nosotros

140

> *Michael, Gloria and I sing well.*

The subjects *Michael, Gloria and I* could be replaced by the pronoun *we*, so that you must use the 1ˢᵗ person plural form of the verb.

2ᴺᴰ PERSON PLURAL — The subject can be expressed in one of two ways:

1. the second person plural pronoun **vosotros** or **vosotras** *you*

> Vosotras **cantáis** bien.
> *You sing well.*

150

2. a multiple subject in which the speaker is included

> Juan y tú **cantáis** muy bien.
> *John and you sing very well.*

In this sentence *John* (whom you would address with the **tú** form) and *you* (whom you also address with the **tú** form) could be replaced by the pronoun *you*, so that you must use the 2ⁿᵈ person plural form of the verb.

160

The familiar plural you form of the verb (the **vosotros** form) is used only in Spain when you are speaking to two or more persons with whom you would use **tú** individually. Many beginning Spanish textbooks do not emphasize or practice the **vosotros** form. Your instructor will inform you if you need to learn the **vosotros** forms of verbs or not.

3ᴺᴰ PERSON PLURAL — The subject can be expressed in one of four ways:

1. the 3ʳᵈ person plural masculine pronoun **ellos** *(they)* and the 3ʳᵈ person plural feminine pronoun **ellas** *(they)*

Ellos cantan muy bien.
They sing very well.

170

Ellas cantan muy bien.
They sing very well.

2. the plural pronoun **ustedes** *(you)*

Elena y Francisco, ustedes cantan muy bien.
Helen and Francis, you sing very well.

In this sentence Helen (whom you would address with the **tú** form) and Francis (whom you would also address with the **tú** form) could be replaced by the **ustedes** form of *you*, so that you must use the 3ʳᵈ person plural form of the verb.

180

The pronoun **ustedes** is generally abbreviated as **Uds.** The abbreviation is used far more frequently than the entire word.

3. two or more proper or common nouns

Isabel, Gloria y Roberto cantan muy bien.
fem. + fem. + masc.   (ellos)
Isabel, Gloria and Robert sing very well.

La chica y su padre cantan muy bien.
fem.   +   masc. (ellos)

190

The girl and her father sing very well.

4. a plural noun

Las chicas cantan muy bien.
fem. pl.   (ellas)
The girls sing very well.

Just as the subject pronoun *it* has no Spanish equivalent, the subject pronoun *they* has no Spanish equivalent when it does not refer to persons (see *What is a Subject Pronoun?*, p. 27).

200

María tiene dos párajos. **Cantan** muy bien.
Mary has two birds. They sing very well.

───────────── **HOW TO CONJUGATE A VERB** ─────────────

A Spanish verb, whether regular or irregular, is composed of two parts:

1. the **STEM**, also called the "root," is the part of the verb left after dropping the last two letters from the infinitive form of the verb (see *What is the Infinitive?*, p. 20).

210

INFINITIVE	STEM
cantar	cant-
comer	com-
vivir	viv-

In regular verbs the stem usually remains the same throughout a conjugation. However, in certain verbs called **STEM-CHANGING VERBS**, the stem will change in a minor way. (Your textbook will identify these verbs.)

2. the **ENDING** which is added to the stem and which changes for each person in the conjugation of regular and irregular verbs.

Regular verbs are divided into three **GROUPS**, also called **CON-JUGATIONS**, identified by the infinitive ending of the verb.

-ar	-er	-ir
1st group	2nd group	3rd group

Each of the three verb groups has its own set of endings for each tense (see *What is Meant by Tense?*, p. 56). Memorizing the conjugation of one sample verb for each group enables you to conjugate all the other regular verbs belonging to that group.

As an example of the steps to follow to conjugate a regular verb, let us look at verbs of the 1st group (-**ar** verbs); that is, verbs like **hablar** *(to speak)* and **tomar** *(to take)* that follow the pattern of **cantar** *(to sing)* conjugated on p. 36.

1. Identify the group of the verb by its infinitive ending.

hablar
tomar   → -**ar** verbs or 1st conjugation or group

2. Find the verb stem by removing the infinitive ending.

habl-
tom-

3. Add the ending that agrees with the subject.

yo	hablo	yo	tomo
tú	hablas	tú	tomas
él		él	
ella	} habla	ella	} toma
usted		usted	
nosotros		nosotros	
nosotras	} hablamos	nosotras	} tomamos

220

230

240

250

vosotros ⎫ habláis	vosotros ⎫ tomáis
vosotras ⎭	vosotras ⎭

ellos ⎫	ellos ⎫
ellas ⎬ hablan	ellas ⎬ toman
ustedes ⎭	ustedes ⎭

The endings of regular verbs belonging to the other groups are different, but the process of conjugation is the same. Just follow the three steps above.

As irregular verbs are introduced in your textbook, their entire conjugation will be given. Be sure to memorize them because many common verbs are irregular (**tener**, *to have*; **ser**, *to be*; **ir**, *to go*; **hacer**, *to make*, for example).

─────────── **OMITTING THE SUBJECT PRONOUN** ───────────

As you can see, in Spanish, the verb ending indicates the subject. For instance, **hablo** can only have **yo** *(I)* as a subject. When the verb ending indicates the subject, the subject pronoun is often omitted.

hablo	*I speak*
hablas	*you speak*
hablamos	*we speak*
habláis	*you speak*

However, to avoid confusion it is often necessary to include the pronoun in the 3ʳᵈ person singular and plural.

	él habla	*he speaks*
habla could be	ella habla	*she speaks*
	Ud. habla	*you speak*
	ellos hablan	*they speak*
hablan could be	ellas hablan	*they speak*
	Uds. hablan	*you speak*

─ *REVIEW* ─

Write the stem and conjugate the regular verb **comprar** *(to buy)*.

STEM: _____

yo _____	nosotros_____
tú _____	vosotros _____
él	ellos
ella _____	ellas _____
Ud.	Uds.

260

270

280

CHAPTER

12

WHAT ARE AUXILIARY VERBS?

A verb is called an AUXILIARY VERB or HELPING VERB when
   it helps another verb, called the MAIN VERB,
   form one of its tenses.

He *has been gone* two weeks.	*has*	AUXILIARY VERB
	been	AUXILIARY VERB
	gone	MAIN VERB

IN ENGLISH

There are three auxiliary verbs, *to have, to be*, and *to do*,
as well as a series of auxiliary words such as *will, would,
may, must, can, could* that are used to change the tense
and meaning of the main verb.

- Auxiliaries are used primarily to indicate the tense of
  the main verb (present, past, future — see *What is Meant
  by Tense?*, p. 56).

    Mary *is reading* a book. PRESENT
    auxiliary *to be*

    Mary *has read* a book. PAST
    auxiliary *to have*

    Mary *will read* a book. FUTURE
    auxiliary *will*

- The auxiliary verb *to do* is used to help formulate questions and to make sentences negative (see *What are
  Declarative and Interrogative Sentences?*, p. 48 and *What
  are Affirmative and Negative Sentences?*, p. 45).

    Does Mary *read* a book? INTERROGATIVE SENTENCE
    Mary *does not read* a book. NEGATIVE SENTENCE

IN SPANISH

There are three verbs that can be used as auxiliary verbs:
estar *(to be)*, **haber** *(to have)*, and **ser** *(to be)*. The other
English auxiliaries such as *do, does, did, will*, or *would* do
not exist as auxiliaries in Spanish. Their meaning is con-
veyed either by a different structure or by the form of the
main verb. You will find more on this topic under the different tenses.

A verb tense composed of an auxiliary verb plus a main verb is called a COMPOUND TENSE, as opposed to a SIMPLE TENSE which is a tense composed of only the main verb.

> Julia **estudia.**
> |
> simple tense
> present of **estudiar**
> *Julia studies.*

> Julia **ha estudiado.**
> | |
> auxiliary main
> verb   verb
> compound tense
> perfect of **estudiar**
> *Julia has studied.*

—— AUXILIARY VERBS ARE USED TO INDICATE TENSE AND VOICE ——

The auxiliary verbs **estar, haber,** and **ser** conjugated in the different tenses are followed by the participle of the main verb (see *What is a Participle?*, p. 63) to form three types of compound tenses in Spanish.

Let us look at examples of some compound tenses.

PERFECT TENSES — The auxiliary verb **haber** *(to have)* followed by the past participle of the main verb is used to form the many perfect tenses (see *What is a Participle?*, p. 63 and *What are the Perfect Tenses?*, p. 79).

- perfect tense → present tense of **haber** + past participle of main verb

> Los estudiantes **han llegado.**
> | |
> auxiliary main
> verb   verb
> **haber**   **llegar** *(to arrive)*
> *The students **have arrived.***

- pluperfect tense → imperfect tense of **haber** + past participle of main verb

> Los estudiantes ya **habían llegado.**
> | |
> auxiliary main
> verb   verb
> **haber**   **llegar** *(to arrive)*
> *The students **had already arrived.***

You will learn other perfect tenses as your study of Spanish progresses.

CONTINUOUS TENSES — The auxiliary verb **estar** *(to be)* followed by the present participle of the main verb is used to form the continuous tenses (see *What is a Participle?*, p. 63 and *What are the Continuous Tenses?*, p. 66).

■ present continuous tense → present tense of **estar** + present participle of main verb

> **Estoy leyendo** un libro ahora.
>   auxiliary main
>   verb   verb
>   estar   leer *(to read)*
> *I am reading a book now.*

■ imperfect continuous tense → imperfect tense of **estar** + present participle of main verb

> **Estábamos escuchando** la radio.
>   auxiliary   main
>   verb   verb
>   estar   escuchar *(to listen)*
> *We were listening to the radio.*

You will learn other continuous tenses as your study of Spanish progresses.

PASSIVE VOICE — The auxiliary verb **ser** *(to be)* is used to form the true passive voice (see *What is Meant by Active and Passive Voice?*, p. 91).

> El puente **fue construido** por los romanos.
>   auxiliary main verb
>   ser   construir *(to build)*
> *The bridge was constructed by the Romans.*

— *R E V I E W* —

Circle the auxiliary verbs in the following sentences.
■ Cross out the English auxiliaries that are not used as auxiliaries in Spanish.

1. We will go to Peru this year.

2. What are you doing?

3. Did you write your parents this week?

4. Tom had already graduated from high school by age sixteen.

5. Do you want to go to the movies with us?

WHAT ARE AFFIRMATIVE AND NEGATIVE SENTENCES?

A sentence can be classified according
to whether or not the verb is negated,
that is, made negative with the word *not* or
another negative word such as *never, nobody*, or *nothing*.

An **AFFIRMATIVE SENTENCE** is a sentence whose verb is not
negated. It states a fact that is.

> Spain is a country in Europe.
> John will work in the university.
> They liked to travel.

A **NEGATIVE SENTENCE** is a sentence whose verb is negated
with a negative word such as *no, not, never*. It states that a
fact or situation is not true; it denies or negates the information it contains.

> Spain is *not* a country in Latin America.
> John will *not* work in a factory.
> They *never* liked to travel.

IN ENGLISH ─────────────────────────────

An affirmative sentence can be changed to a negative sentence in one of two ways:

1. by adding *not* after forms of the verb *to be*, auxiliary verbs,
   or auxiliary words (see *What are Auxiliary Verbs?*, p. 42)

AFFIRMATIVE	NEGATIVE
John *is* a student.	John is *not* a student.
Mary *can* do it.	Mary can*not* do it.
They *will* travel.	They will *not* travel.

   Frequently, the word *not* is attached to the verb and the
   letter "o" is replaced by an apostrophe; this is called a
   CONTRACTION: *is not → isn't; cannot → can't; will not → won't.*

2. by adding the auxiliary verb *do, does*, or *did + not +* the
   dictionary form of the main verb (*do* or *does* is used for
   negatives in the present tense and *did* for negatives in
   the past tense—see *What is the Present Tense?*, p. 58 and
   What is the Past Tense?, p. 60)

1

10

20

30

AFFIRMATIVE	NEGATIVE
We *study* a lot.	We *do not* study a lot.
Julia *writes* well.	Julia *does not* write well.
The plane *arrived.*	The plane *did not* arrive.

Frequently, *do, does,* or *did* is contracted with *not: do not* → *don't; does not* → *doesn't; did not* → *didn't.*

IN SPANISH ────────────────────────────────

The basic rule for turning an affirmative sentence into a negative sentence is much more simple than in English. You merely place **no** in front of the conjugated verb.

AFFIRMATIVE	NEGATIVE
Estudiamos mucho.	No estudiamos mucho.
	| conjugated verb
*We **study** a lot.*	*We **do not** study a lot.*
Julia **escribe** bien.	Julia **no** escribe bien.
	| conjugated verb
*Julia **writes** well.*	*Julia **does not** write well.*
El avión **llegó.**	El avión **no** llegó.
	| conjugated verb
*The plane **arrived.***	*The plane **didn't** arrive.*

CAREFUL — Remember that there is no equivalent for the auxiliary words *do, does, did* in Spanish; do not try to include them in negative sentences.

──────────────── **NEGATIVE WORDS** ────────────────

In both English and Spanish there are negative words that can be added to an affirmative sentence.

IN ENGLISH

The most common negative words are: *nothing, nobody, no one, never.*

> I have *nothing* for you.
> He *never* arrives on time.
> When John is angry, he speaks to *no one (nobody)*.

IN SPANISH

The most common negative words are **nada** *(nothing)*, **nadie** *(nobody, no one)*, and **nunca** *(never)*. Often the negative word is used with **no** in the same sentence.

No tengo **nada** para ti.
*I have **nothing** for you. (I don't have **anything** for you.)*

Nunca llega a tiempo.
*He **never** arrives on time.*

Cuando Juan está enojado, no le habla a **nadie**.
*When John is angry, he speaks to **no one** (**nobody**).*

The position of the negative word can change according to its function in the sentence. (See *What are Indefinites and Negatives?*, p. 178.)

──────────── NEGATIVE ANSWERS ────────────

IN ENGLISH

When answering a question negatively in English, both *no* and *not* will often appear in the answer.

Do you live near the park? *No*, I do *not* live near the park.

IN SPANISH

Since both *no* and *not* have the Spanish equivalent **no**, the word **no** will appear twice in the negative answer to the above question in Spanish.

¿Vives cerca del parque? **No, no** vivo cerca del parque.
                               | |
                             no not

*Do you live near the park? **No**, I do **not** live near the park.*

── *REVIEW* ──

Write the negative of each sentence.
- Circle the words which indicate the negative in the sentences you have just written.
- Place an "x" over the words that would not appear in the Spanish negative sentence.

1. We want to leave class early.

   _____

2. He did his homework yesterday.

   _____

3. Teresa will go to Chile this summer.

   _____

4. Robert can go to the restaurant with us.

   _____

CHAPTER

14

WHAT ARE DECLARATIVE AND INTERROGATIVE SENTENCES?

A sentence can be classified as to whether it is making a statement or asking a question.

A DECLARATIVE SENTENCE is a sentence that makes a statement.

Columbus discovered America in 1492.

An INTERROGATIVE SENTENCE is a sentence that asks a question.

Did Columbus discover America in 1492?

In written language, an interrogative sentence always ends with a question mark.

IN ENGLISH ─────────────────────────────

A declarative sentence can be changed to an interrogative sentence in one of two ways:

1. by adding the auxiliary verb *do, does,* or *did* before the subject and changing the main verb to the dictionary form of the verb (*do* and *does* are used to introduce a question in the present tense and *did* to introduce a question in the past tense — see *What is the Present Tense?*, p. 58 and *What is the Past Tense?*, p. 60)

DECLARATIVE SENTENCE	INTERROGATIVE SENTENCE
Philip *likes* sport cars.	*Does* Philip *like* sport cars?
present 3rd pers. sing.	present 3rd pers. sing. + dictionary form
Paul and Mary *sing* well.	*Do* Paul and Mary *sing* well?
present 3rd pers. pl.	present 3rd pers. pl. + dictionary form
Mark *went* to Mexico.	*Did* Mark *go* to Mexico?
past	past + dictionary form

2. by inverting the normal word order of subject + verb to verb + subject. This INVERSION process can only be used with forms of the verb *to be,* auxiliary verbs or auxiliary words (see *What are Auxiliary Verbs?*, p. 42).

DECLARATIVE SENTENCE	INTERROGATIVE SENTENCE
Paul is home.	*Is Paul* home?
subject + verb *to be*	verb + subject
You have received a letter.	*Have you received* a letter?
subject + *to have* + main verb	*to have* + subject + main verb
She will come tomorrow.	*Will she come* tomorrow?
subject + *will* + main verb	*will* + subject + main verb

IN SPANISH

A declarative sentence can be changed to an interrogative sentence by using the inversion process.

In a simple declarative sentence that consists of a subject + verb, the word order of the question is verb + subject.

DECLARATIVE SENTENCE	INTERROGATIVE SENTENCE
Juan estudia.	¿Estudia Juan?
subject verb	verb subject
John studies.	*Does John study?*
Los niños cantan.	¿Cantan los niños?
subject verb	verb subject
The children sing.	*Do the children sing?*

Notice that in written Spanish the question is signalled at both the beginning and end of the sentence. The punctuation mark at the beginning of the sentence looks like an upside-down question mark (¿); a question mark like the one in English is located at the end of the sentence (?).

TAG QUESTIONS

In both English and Spanish when you expect a yes-or-no answer, you can also transform a statement into a question by adding a short phrase at the end of the statement. This short phrase is called a TAG or TAG QUESTION.

IN ENGLISH

There are different tags, depending on the tense of the verb of the statement and whether the statement is affirmative or negative. For instance, affirmative statements take negative tags and negative statements take affirmative tags.

John and Mary *are* friends, *aren't they?*
affirmative statement   negative tag

John and Mary *aren't* friends, *are they?*

negative statement   affirmative tag

IN SPANISH

The words **¿no?**, **¿verdad?**, or **¿no es verdad?** can be added to the end of an affirmative statement to form a tag question.

> Juan y María son amigos, **¿no?**
> *John and Mary are friends, **aren't they?***

> Trabajas mucho, **¿verdad?**
> *You work hard, **don't you?***

> Hoy es miércoles, **¿no es verdad?**
> *Today is Wednesday, **isn't it?***

The word **¿verdad?** is generally added to the end of a negative statement to form a tag question.

> Juan y María no son amigos, **¿verdad?**
> *John and Mary aren't friends, **are they?***

— REVIEW —

A. Using the inversion process, write the interrogative form of each declarative sentence on the line provided.
- In the interrogative sentence, circle the English words that indicate the interrogative.
- In the interrogative sentence, put an "x" over the words that would not appear in the Spanish question.

1. Richard and Kathy studied all evening.

_____

2. Your brother eats a lot.

_____

3. The girl's parents speak Spanish.

_____

B. Change the sentence to an interrogative sentence using a tag.

My mother and father went to the movies.

_____

WHAT ARE SOME EQUIVALENTS OF "TO BE"?

IN ENGLISH

The verb *to be* has the following forms in the present tense: *I am; you are; he, she, it is; we are; you are; they are.* It is used in a variety of ways:

- to tell time

    It *is* 4:00.

- to discuss health

    John *isn't* very well.

- to describe traits and characteristics

    Mary *is* tall and blond.

- to tell ages

    I *am* twenty years old.

- to explain what there is or there are in specific places

    There *are* twenty-five students in the class.

IN SPANISH

There are various verbs used to express the English verb *to be:*

ENGLISH	SPANISH
	1. **ser** *(to be)*
to be	2. **estar** *(to be)*
	3. **tener** *(to have)*
there is, there are	4. **hay** (a form of *to have*)

Depending on what you want to say, you will have to use one of these four verbs. Here are a few rules to help you select the correct one:

1. **TO BE = "SER"**

    Use a form of the verb **ser** when you are speaking about the following:

    - to tell time

        It is 4:00.
        Son las cuatro.

- to show possession

  That car is John's.
  Ese coche **es** de Juan.

  This book is yours.
  Este libro **es** tuyo.

⁴⁰

- to express nationality and origin

  Mary is Spanish; she is from Madrid.
  María **es** española; **es** de Madrid.

- with nouns to identify someone or something

  Mr. Robles is a lawyer.
  El señor Robles **es** abogado.

  That building is the language laboratory.
  Ese edificio **es** el laboratorio de lenguas.

⁵⁰

- with adjectives to describe traits or characteristics

  Mary is tall and blond.
  María **es** alta y rubia.

2. To be = "Estar"

Use a form of the verb **estar** when you are speaking about the following:

- to express location

  *John and I **are** in the library.*
  Juan y yo **estamos** en la biblioteca.

⁶⁰

  *The books **are** on the table.*
  Los libros **están** sobre la mesa.

- to discuss health

  *How **are** you?*
  ¿Cómo **está** Ud.?

  Mary is fine but John is sick.
  María **está** bien pero Juan **está** enfermo.

- with adjectives that describe a condition

  *I **am** tired and worried.*
⁷⁰
  adjectives of condition
  Estoy cansada y preocupada.

"Ser" vs. "Estar"

As you can see above, when the verb *to be* is followed by an adjective, both **ser** and **estar** can be used. You will need to decide what type of adjective is used in order to select the appropriate verb.

- with adjectives that describe physical characteristics and personality traits → **ser**

  My house is modern.
  |
  characteristic
  Mi casa **es** moderna.

  80

  Ser is used because the adjective *modern* distinguishes the house from others. It answers the question: Which house is yours? or What is your house like?

  Mary is nice.
  |
  trait
  María **es** simpática.

  Ser is used because the adjective *nice* distinguishes Mary from other persons. It answers the question: What kind of person is Mary?

  90

- adjectives that describe conditions → **estar**

  My house is dirty.
  |
  condition
  Mi casa **está** sucia.

  Estar is used because *dirty* describes a condition, not a normal characteristic of the house. It answers the question: What condition is the house in?

  100

  Mary is tired.
  |
  condition
  María **está** cansada.

  Estar is used because the adjective *tired* describes a condition, not a normal characteristic of Mary. It answers the question: What is Mary's condition?

In a question, a different type of information is being requested depending on whether **ser** or **estar** is used.

  ¿Cómo **es** María?

  Use of **ser** → What is Mary like? What are her traits?

  110

  ¿Cómo **está** María?

  Use of **estar** → How is Mary? What is her condition? How is she feeling?

3. To be = "Tener" *(to have)*

Sometimes the English expression *to be* + adjective is expressed with the Spanish verb *to have* (**tener**) + noun. These expressions using **tener** + noun must be memorized.

Here are a few examples:

120

I am hungry.
|
"to be" + adjective
Tengo hambre.
|
"to have" + noun [I *have* hunger.]

I am twenty years old.
| |
"to be"   +   adjective
Tengo veinte años.
| |
"to have" + noun [word-for-word: I *have* twenty years]

4. THERE IS, THERE ARE = "HAY"

130

The English expressions *there is* or *there are* are translated with the Spanish word **hay**. **Hay** is INVARIABLE; that is, it does not change form since it can be either singular or plural.

There is a book on the table.
      |
     singular noun
Hay un libro sobre la mesa.

There are many books on the table.
        |

140

     plural noun
Hay muchos libros sobre la mesa.

You must learn to use this common expression correctly and not confuse it with **estar**. To avoid using the wrong verb, see if you can replace the "is" or "are" of the English sentence with "there is" or "there are". If you can, you must use **hay**; if you can't, then **está** or **están** must be used.

On the table is a book.
      |
    there is (you can say: On the table *there is* a book.)

150

    hay (to show presence)

The book is on the table.
     |
    is (you can't say: The book *there is* on the table.)
 |
   está (to show location)

In the classroom are students.
       |
there are (you can say: In the classroom *there are* students.)
   |
   hay (to show presence)

*The chairs and tables **are** in the classroom.* 160
    |
are (you can't say: The chairs and the table *there are* in the
    | classroom.)
están (to show location)

— *REVIEW* —

A. Decide if the italicized words are adjectives that describe a characteristic (CR) or a condition (CN).
- Circle the infinitive form of the verb you would use in Spanish, **ser** or **estar**.

1. My car is *gray*.   CR   CN   ser estar

2. My car is *clean*.   CR   CN   ser estar

3. The students are *worried*.   CR   CN   ser estar

4. John is *tall, dark, and handsome*.   CR   CN   ser estar

5. I am *bored*.   CR   CN   ser estar

6. John, are you *sick?*   CR   CN   ser estar

7. Mary and I are *blond*.   CR   CN   ser estar

B. Decide if the words *is* or *are* express location (L) or express the presence (P) of people or things.
- Circle the correct Spanish equivalent of the above: **estar** or **hay**.

1. Our cars are in the garage.   L   P   estar hay

2. In the garage are several bicycles. L   P   estar hay

3. Your lunch is on the table.   L   P   estar hay

4. For your lunch there is some soup.   L   P   estar hay

CHAPTER

16

WHAT IS MEANT BY TENSE?

The TENSE of a verb indicates when the action of the verb takes place: at the present time, in the past, or in the future. The word *tense* comes from the same word as the Spanish word "tiempo," which means *time*.

I am studying PRESENT
I studied   PAST
I shall study FUTURE

As you can see in the above examples, just by putting the verb in a different tense and without giving any additional information (such as "I am studying *now*," "I studied *yesterday*," "I shall study *tomorrow*"), you can indicate when the action of the verb takes place.

Tenses may be classified according to the way they are formed. A SIMPLE TENSE consists of only one verb form (I *studied*), while a COMPOUND TENSE consists of one or more auxiliaries plus the main verb (I *am studying*).

In this section we will only consider tenses of the indicative mood (see *What is Meant by Mood?*, p. 69).

IN ENGLISH ————————————————————————

Listed below are the main tenses of the indicative mood whose equivalents you will encounter in Spanish:

PRESENT
I study   PRESENT
I do study   PRESENT EMPHATIC
I am studying PRESENT CONTINUOUS

PAST
I studied   SIMPLE PAST (PAST DEFINITE)
I did study   PAST EMPHATIC
I have studied PERFECT
I was studying PAST CONTINUOUS
I had studied PLUPERFECT

FUTURE
I shall study   FUTURE
I shall have studied FUTURE PERFECT

CONDITIONAL
I would study   CONDITIONAL
I would have studied CONDITIONAL PERFECT

As you can see, there are only two simple tenses (present and simple past). All of the other tenses are compound tenses.

IN SPANISH ————————————————————————

Listed below are the main tenses of the indicative mood that you will encounter in Spanish.

PRESENT

| estudio | *I study, I do study*
I am studying | PRESENT |
| estoy estudiando | *I am studying* | PRESENT CONTINUOUS |

PAST

estudié	*I studied, I did study*	PRETERITE
estudiaba	*I used to study* *I was studying*	IMPERFECT
estaba estudiando	*I was studying*	IMPERFECT CONTINUOUS
he estudiado	*I have studied*	PERFECT
había estudiado	*I had studied*	PLUPERFECT

FUTURE

| estudiaré | *I shall study* | FUTURE |
| habré estudiado | *I shall have studied* | FUTURE PERFECT |

CONDITIONAL[1]

| estudiaría | *I would study* | CONDITIONAL |
| habría estudiado | *I would have studied* | CONDITIONAL PERFECT |

As you can see, there are more simple tenses than in English (present, preterite, imperfect, future, and conditional). The compound tenses in Spanish are formed with the auxiliary verbs **estar** *(to be)* or **haber** *(to have)* + the main verb.

This handbook discusses the various tenses and their usage in separate chapters: *What is the Present Tense?*, p. 58; *What is the Past Tense?*, p. 60; *What is the Future Tense?*, p. 83; *What is the Conditional?*, p. 86; *What are the Continuous Tenses?*, p. 66; *What are the Perfect Tenses?*, p. 79. Verb tenses can be grouped according to the mood in which they are used (see *What is Meant by Mood?*, p. 69).

CAREFUL — Do not assume that tenses with the same name are used in the same way in English and in Spanish.

---

[1]The conditional tenses have been included because they have parallels in English. The subjunctive tenses have been omitted because they have no parallels in English.

CHAPTER

17

WHAT IS THE PRESENT TENSE?

The PRESENT TENSE indicates that the action is happening at the present time. It can be at the moment the speaker is speaking, a habitual action, or a general truth.

> I *see* you.
> He *smokes* when he *is* nervous.
> The sun *rises* every day.

IN ENGLISH

There are three forms of the verb that indicate the present tense. Each form has a slightly different meaning:

Mary *studies* in the library.	PRESENT
Mary *is studying* in the library.	PRESENT CONTINUOUS
Mary *does study* in the library.	PRESENT EMPHATIC

Depending on the way a question is worded, you will automatically choose one of the three above forms.

> Where does Mary study? She *studies* in the library.
> Where is Mary now? She *is studying* in the library.
> Does Mary study in the library? Yes, she *does [study* in the library].

IN SPANISH

The present tense in Spanish is a simple tense formed by adding a set of endings to the stem of the verb (see *What is a Verb Conjugation?*, p. 35). Your textbook will give you the present tense endings.

Unlike English, there is only one verb form to indicate the present tense. The Spanish present tense is used to express the meaning of the English present, present continuous, and present emphatic tenses.

*Mary **studies** in the library.*
                    |
            estudia

*Mary **is studying** in the library.*
            └──┬──┘
            estudia

*Mary **does study** in the library.*
            └──┬──┘
                estudia

CAREFUL — The present is always indicated by the ending of the verb without an auxiliary verb such as *is* and *does*. You must not translate these English auxiliary verbs. Simply put ⁴⁰ the main verb in the present tense.

— *REVIEW* —

Fill in the proper form of the verb *to read* in the following answers.
▪ Write the Spanish verb form for sentences 2, 3 and 4.

1. What does Mary do all day?

   She _____.

   SPANISH VERB: **lee.**

2. What is Mary doing now?

   She_____.

   SPANISH VERB: _____

3. Does Mary read Spanish?

   Yes, she _____ Spanish.

   SPANISH VERB: _____

4. Has she read *Don Quixote?*

   No, but, she_____ it right now.

   SPANISH VERB: _____

CHAPTER

18

WHAT IS THE PAST TENSE?

The **PAST TENSE** is used to express an action
that occurred in the past.

I *saw* you yesterday.

IN ENGLISH

There are several verb forms that indicate the action took
place in the past.

I worked	SIMPLE PAST (PAST DEFINITE)
I was working	PAST CONTINUOUS
I used to work	WITH HELPING VERB USED TO
I did work	PAST EMPHATIC
I have worked	PERFECT
I had worked	PLUPERFECT

The simple past is a simple tense; that is, it consists of one
word (*worked* in the example above). The other past tenses
are compound tenses; that is, they consist of more than
one word—an auxiliary plus a main verb *(was working, did
work)*. The perfect and pluperfect tenses are discussed in a
separate section (see *What are the Perfect Tenses?*, p. 79).

IN SPANISH

As in English, there are several verb tenses that indicate
that an action took place in the past. Each tense has its
own set of endings and its own rules that tell us when and
how to use it. We are concerned here with only two of the
past tenses in Spanish: the preterite (**el pretérito**) and the
imperfect (**el imperfecto**).

THE PRETERITE

The preterite is a simple tense formed by adding a set of
endings to the stem of the verb. There are many irregular
verbs in the preterite tense. It is very important to learn
the preterite forms given in your textbook since the stems
of the preterite are also used as the base for other verb
forms.

The preterite generally translates as the simple past in
English.

hablé	*I spoke*
estudié	*I studied*

THE IMPERFECT

The imperfect is also a simple tense formed by adding a set of endings to the stem of the verb. The conjugation is very regular (there are only three irregular verbs in the imperfect tense).

There are two English verb forms that indicate that the imperfect should be used in Spanish.

1. the English verb form includes, or could include, *used to*

>   *When I was little, **I played** in the park.*

>   could be replaced by *used to play*

>   Cuando yo era joven, **jugaba** en el parque.

>   imperfect

2. the English verb form is in the past continuous tense, as in *was playing, were studying*

>   *I was studying in my room.*
>   Yo **estudiaba** en mi cuarto.

>   imperfect

Except for these two verb forms, the English verb will not indicate to you whether you should use the imperfect or the preterite.

SELECTION OF THE PRETERITE OR IMPERFECT

When discussing and describing past events and activities, both the imperfect and preterite are used. Whether to put a verb in the preterite or the imperfect often depends upon the context. As a general guideline, the difference in the two tenses is as follows:

> PRETERITE ⟶   tells "what happened" during a fixed period of time

> IMPERFECT ⟶   tells "how things used to be" or "what was going on" during a period of time

Here is an example. The same form of the verb *to go,* namely "went," is used in the two answers below: "I *went* to the park." However, the tense of the Spanish verb **ir** *(to go)* changes depending on the question asked.

▪ "What happened?"

>   QUESTION: *What **did** you **do** yesterday?*
>   ANSWER: *I **went** to the park.*

>   The question and answer tell "what happened yesterday;" therefore, the Spanish equivalent of *did do* and *went* are in the preterite.

40

50

60

70

80

QUESTION: ¿Qué **hiciste** ayer?
ANSWER: **Fui** al parque.

- **"How things used to be"**

  QUESTION: *What did you do when you were a child?*
  ANSWER: *I went to the park.*
  > The question and answer tell "how things used to be;" therefore, the Spanish equivalent of *did do* and *went* are in the imperfect.

  QUESTION: ¿Qué **hacías** cuando eras joven?
  ANSWER: **Iba** al parque.

- **"What was going on?"**

  The imperfect and the preterite indicate actions that took place during the same time period in the past. You will often find the two tenses intermingled in a sentence or a story.

  I was reading when he arrived.
  > Both actions *reading* and *arrived* took place at the same time. What was going on? *I was reading* → imperfect. What happened? *He arrived* → preterite.

  Leía cuando **llegó.**
    | |
  imperfect   preterite

Consult your Spanish textbook for additional guidelines to help you choose the appropriate tense.

— *REVIEW* —

Circle the verbs that would be put in the imperfect and underline the verbs that would be put in the preterite in Spanish.

Last summer, I *went* to Mexico with my family. Everyone *was* very excited when we *arrived* at the airport. While my mother *was checking* the luggage and my father *was handling* the tickets, my little sister Mary *ran* away. My parents *dropped* everything and *tried* to catch her, but she *ducked* behind the counter. Finally, a manager *grabbed* her and *brought* her back to us. She *was crying* because she *was* sad she *was leaving* her dog Heidi for two weeks. Everyone *comforted* her and, finally, she *smiled* and *got on* the plane.

WHAT IS A PARTICIPLE?

A **PARTICIPLE** is a form of a verb that can be used [1]
in one of two ways: with an auxiliary verb to indicate
certain tenses, or as an adjective to describe something.

He *has closed* the door.
| |
auxiliary + participle → past tense

He heard me through the *closed* door.
|
participle describing *door* → adjective

There are two types of participles: the present participle
and the past participle. [10]

────────────── **PRESENT PARTICIPLE** ──────────────

IN ENGLISH

The present participle is easy to recognize because it is the
-ing form of the verb: *working, studying, dancing, playing.*

The present participle has two primary uses:

1. as the main verb in compound tenses with the auxiliary
verb *to be* to indicate a continuous tense (see *What are
the Continuous Tenses?*, p. 66) [20]

She *is writing* with her new pen.
present continuous of *to write*

They *were sleeping.*
past continuous of *to sleep*

2. as an adjective (see *What are Descriptive Adjectives?*, p. 97)

The pen is a *writing* instrument.
|
describes the noun *instrument*

He woke the *sleeping* child. [30]
|
describes the noun *child*

IN SPANISH

The present participle can be regular or irregular. Here are
the endings of regular verbs:

1. **-ar** verbs add **-ando** to the stem (see p. 39)
2. **-er** and **-ir** verbs add **-iendo** to the stem

The **-ndo** of the Spanish participle corresponds to the *-ing* of the English present participle.

Here are examples of regular present participles:

INFINITIVE	STEM	PRESENT PARTICIPLE
cant**ar**	cant-	cant**ando**
com**er**	com-	com**iendo**
viv**ir**	viv-	viv**iendo**

There are some irregular forms that you will have to memorize individually. The present participle is used primarily in the formation of the continuous tenses (see *What are the Continuous Tenses?*, p. 66).

CAREFUL — Never assume that an English word ending in *-ing* will translate by its Spanish counterpart in **-ndo**.

PAST PARTICIPLE

IN ENGLISH

The past participle is formed in several ways. It is the form of the verb that follows *I have*: *I have **spoken**, I have **written**, I have **walked**.*

The past participle has two primary uses:

1. as the main verb in compound tenses with the auxiliary verb *to have*

> I *have written* all that I have to say.
> perfect of *to write*

> He *hasn't spoken* to me since our quarrel.
> perfect of *to speak*

2. as an adjective

> Is the *written* word more important than the *spoken* word?
> describes the noun *word*   describes the noun *word*

IN SPANISH

The past participle can be regular or irregular. Here are the endings of regular verbs:

1. **-ar** verbs add **-ado** to the stem
2. **-er** and **-ir** verbs add **-ido** to the stem

The **-do** of the Spanish participle often corresponds to the *-ed* of the English past participle.

Here are examples of regular past participles:

INFINITIVE	STEM	PAST PARTICIPLE
cantar	cant-	cantado
comer	com-	comido
vivir	viv-	vivido

You will have to memorize irregular past participles individually.

As in English, the past participle can be used as the main verb of a compound tense or as an adjective.

1. as the main verb in compound tenses with the auxiliary verb **haber** *(to have)* to indicate a perfect tense (see *What are the Perfect Tenses?*, p. 79)

> Los estudiantes **han terminado** la lección.
> *The students **have finished** the lesson.*

2. as an adjective that agrees with the noun it modifies in gender and number

> the **closed** door
>> *Closed* modifies the noun *door*. Since **la puerta** *(door)* is feminine singular, the word for *closed* must be feminine singular. The participle must end with the letter -a.
>
> la puerta **cerrada**
>
> the **stolen** cars
>> *Stolen* modifies the noun *cars*. Since **los coches** *(cars)* is masculine plural, the word for *stolen* must be masculine plural. The participle must end with the letters -os.
>
> los coches **robados**

— REVIEW —

Identify the verb forms in italics: present participle (P) or past participle (PP).

1. At 10:00 p.m. John was *watching* TV.

    P   PP

2. We had already *gone* when Tom called.

    P   PP

3. An antique dealer near our house fixes *broken* china.

    P   PP

4. Mary is *studying* in the library right now.

    P   PP

CHAPTER

20

WHAT ARE THE CONTINUOUS TENSES?

The **CONTINUOUS TENSES** are used to talk about actions that are in progress at a specific moment in time; they emphasize the moment that an action takes place.

John *is talking* on the phone.

present continuous:
emphasizes that the action is taking place right now

We *were trying* to start the car.

past continuous:
emphasizes that the action was taking place in the past

IN ENGLISH ─────────────────────────────

The continuous tenses are made up of the auxiliary verb *to be* + the present participle of the main verb (see *What is a Participle?*, p. 63).

We *are leaving* right now.

present participle of
main verb *to leave*
present tense of *to be*

At that moment John *was washing* his car.

present participle of
main verb *to wash*
past tense of *to be*

Notice that it is the tense of the auxiliary verb *to be* that indicates when the action of the main verb takes place.

we *are* studying

present tense of *to be* → present continuous

we *were* studying

past tense of *to be* → past continuous

IN SPANISH ─────────────────────────────

The continuous tenses are made up of the auxiliary verb **estar** *(to be)* + the present participle of the main verb. All the tenses in Spanish have a continuous form. In this section we shall only study the present continuous.

The present continuous is made up of the present tense of **estar** + the present participle of the main verb.

Estamos saliendo ahora mismo.

present tense　present participle
of **estar**　　of **salir** *(to leave)*

We are leaving right now.

¿**Estás comiendo** ahora?

present tense　present participle
of **estar**　　of **comer** *(to eat)*

Are you eating now?

―――――――― **USE OF THE CONTINUOUS TENSES** ――――――――

The continuous tenses are used far more frequently in English than in Spanish.

In English, the continuous tenses are used for habitual actions, to state general truths, or to indicate that an action is happening at a specific moment (see *What is the Present Tense?*, p. 58).

In Spanish, the continuous tenses are only used for emphasis, for instance, to emphasize that an action is taking place at a particular moment, as opposed to another time, or to stress the continuity of an action. Where English uses the present continuous tense, Spanish often uses the present tense.

*John, what **are you studying** in school?*

English present continuous → Spanish present: **estudias**
You are asking what John is studying in general
over a period of time.

*John, what **are you studying** now?*

English present continuous → Spanish present continuous:
estás estudiando
The word *now* indicates that you want to know what John is
studying at this particular time as opposed to all other times.

*Mary, **are you working** for the government?*

English present continuous → Spanish present: **trabajas**
You are asking where Mary is working in general
over a period of time.

*Mary, **are you working** right now?*

English present continuous → Spanish present continuous:
estás trabajando
The words *right now* indicate that you want to know if Mary
is working at this particular time as opposed to all other times.

— *REVIEW* —

Indicate whether the Spanish version of the following English sentences would use the present tense (P) or the present continuous (PT).

1. This semester Robert is studying physics.   P   PT

2. Children, why are you making so much noise?   P   PT

3. I can't come to the phone. I am
   getting ready to go out.   P   PT

4. My brother is working for a computer firm
   in California.   P   PT

5. My brother is doing very well.   P   PT

WHAT IS MEANT BY MOOD?

MOOD is the grammatical term for a category of a verb   1
used to indicate the attitude of a speaker
toward what he or she is saying.

Different moods serve different purposes. For example,
verbs that state a fact belong to one mood *(you are studying, you studied)*. The verb form that gives orders belongs
to another mood *(Study!)*. Some moods have multiple
tenses while others have only one tense.

You should recognize the names of the moods so that
you will know what your Spanish textbook is referring to   10
when it uses these terms. You will learn when to use the
various moods as you learn verbs and their tenses.

IN ENGLISH ─────────────────────────────

Verbs can be in one of three moods.

1. The INDICATIVE MOOD is used to state the action of the
   verb, that is, to *indicate* facts. This is the most common
   mood, and most of the verb forms that you use in
   everyday conversation belong to the indicative mood.
   The majority of the tenses studied in this handbook
   belong to the indicative mood: for example, the present   20
   tense (see p. 58), the past tense (see p. 60), and the
   future tense (see p. 83).

   > Robert *studies* Spanish.
   > |
   > present indicative

   > Anita *was* here.
   > |
   > past indicative

   > They *will arrive* tomorrow.
   > └───┬───┘
   > future indicative   30

2. The IMPERATIVE MOOD is used to give commands or orders
   (see *What is the Imperative?*, p. 75). This mood is not
   divided into tenses.

   > Robert, *study* Spanish now!
   > Anita, *be* home on time!

3. The **SUBJUNCTIVE MOOD** is used to express an attitude or feeling toward the action of the verb; it is *subjective* about it (see *What is the Subjunctive?*, p. 71). In English this mood is not divided into tenses.

> The school requires that students *study* Spanish.
> I wish that Anita *were* here.
> The teacher recommends that he *do* his homework.

IN SPANISH ────────────────────

The Spanish language identifies two moods: the indicative and the subjunctive.

1. The **INDICATIVE MOOD,** as in English, is the most common and most of the tenses you will learn belong to this mood.

2. The **SUBJUNCTIVE MOOD** is used much more frequently in Spanish than in English. The Spanish subjunctive has four tenses: present, imperfect, perfect, and pluperfect. In addition, most imperative or command forms are also present subjunctive forms. Textbooks will use the term "present subjunctive" to distinguish that tense from the "present indicative."

When there is no reference to mood, the verb belongs to the most common mood, the indicative.

WHAT IS THE SUBJUNCTIVE?

The SUBJUNCTIVE is a mood used to express a wish, [1]
hope, uncertainty or other similar attitude toward
a fact or an idea. Since it stresses the subject's feelings
about the fact or idea, it is usually *subjective* about them.

> I wish he *were* here.
> | |
> subject's subjunctive
> wish

> The teacher insisted that the homework *be* neat.
> | |
> subject's   subjunctive
> attitude   [10]

IN ENGLISH

The subjunctive verb form is difficult to recognize because
it is spelled like other tenses of the verb: the dictionary
form and the simple past (past definite) tense.

INDICATIVE	SUBJUNCTIVE
He *reads* a lot.	The course requires that he *read* a lot.
indicative present *to read*	subjunctive (same as dictionary form)
I *am* in Detroit right now.	I wish I *were* in Madrid.
indicative present *to be*	subjunctive (same as past tense)

[20]

The subjunctive occurs most commonly in three kinds of
sentences.

1. The subjunctive form of the verb *to be* (***were***), is used in
   the *if clause* of hypothetical sentences (see p. 86 in *What
   is the Conditional?* for an explanation of clauses).

> ⌐ if clause ¬   ⌐ result clause ¬
> If I *were* in Europe now, I would go to Madrid. [30]
> |
>   subjunctive

> ⌐ result clause ¬   ⌐ if clause ¬
> John would run faster, if he *were* in shape.
> |
>   subjunctive

2. The same subjunctive form *were* is used in statements expressing a wish.

> I wish I *were* in Europe right now.
> |
>   subjunctive

> I wish she *were* my teacher.
> |
>   subjunctive

3. The subjunctive form of any verb is used following expressions that ask, urge, demand, request or express necessity.

> She asked that I *come* to see her.
> └──┬──┘ |
> request   subjunctive same as dictionary form

> It is necessary that you *study* a lot.
> └────┬────┘ |
> demand   subjunctive same as dictionary form

IN SPANISH ──────────────────────────

The subjunctive is used very frequently; unfortunately English usage will rarely help you decide where or how to use it in Spanish.

Here are a few suggestions as to how to approach the subjunctive when it is introduced in your Spanish textbook:

- When you learn the conjugation of verbs in the present tense of the subjunctive, it is useful to compare those forms to the present indicative. This will help you to remember what distinguishes one from the other.
- Learn the verbs and expressions that require that the verb which follows be put in the subjunctive.

CAREFUL — It is not the verb or expression itself that is put in the subjunctive; it is the verb that follows.

Here are examples of verbs and expressions that require that the verb which follows be in the subjunctive form.

- a verb of wishing or wanting

> Quiero que Uds. **estudien** mucho.
> | |
> **querer** *(to want)*   **estudiar** *(to study)*
> indicative   subjunctive

> *I want you **to study** a lot.*
> (word-for-word: *I want that **you study** a lot*)

- an expression of doubt or uncertainty

Dudo que Roberto **llegue** hoy.

dudar *(to doubt)*   **llegar** *(to arrive)*
indicative   subjunctive

I doubt that Robert will arrive today.

(word-for-word: *I doubt that Robert arrives today*)

- an impersonal expression (**es** + adjective)

Es posible que **compremos** un coche nuevo.

es + adjective   **comprar** *(to buy)*
indicative   subjunctive

It is possible that we will buy a new car.

(word-for-word: *It is possible that we buy a new car*)

- a verb of advice or command

Te aconsejo que **comas** muchos vegetales.

aconsejar *(to advise)*   **comer** *(to eat)*
indicative   subjunctive

I advise you to eat a lot of vegetables.

(word-for-word: *I advise that you eat a lot of vegetables*)

- an expression of emotion

Siento que Julio **esté** enfermo.

sentir *(to be sorry)* **estar** *(to be)*
indicative   subjunctive

I am sorry that Julio is sick.

CAREFUL — The tense of an English verb will rarely indicate to you if it should use the subjunctive in Spanish. As you can see in the examples above, a variety of English verb forms can take the subjunctive in Spanish.

- infinitive

I want you to study a lot.
Quiero que Uds. **estudien** mucho.

I advise you to eat a lot of vegetables.
Te aconsejo que **comas** muchos vegetales.

- future tense

I doubt that Roberto will arrive today.
Dudo que Roberto **llegue** hoy.

It is possible that we will buy a new car.
Es posible que **compremos** un coche nuevo.

- present indicative

I'm sorry that Julio is sick.
Siento que Julio **esté** enfermo.

— REVIEW —

Indicate the appropriate mood in Spanish for the verbs in italics:
the indicative (I) mood or subjunctive (S) mood.

1. John wants Mary *to go out* with him.   I   S

2. I'm happy that you *got* a good job.   I   S

3. My mother says that Tom *is* a good student.   I   S

4. The doctor suggests that you *take* two aspirins.   I   S

5. It's important for you *to learn* Spanish.   I   S

6. We doubt that he *won* the lottery.   I   S

7. I know that John *lives* in that house.   I   S

WHAT IS THE IMPERATIVE?

The IMPERATIVE is used to give someone an order.

The AFFIRMATIVE IMPERATIVE is an order to do something.

Come here!

The NEGATIVE IMPERATIVE is an order not to do something.

Don't come here!

IN ENGLISH

There are two types of commands, depending on who is told to do, or not to do, something.

1. "YOU" COMMAND — When an order is given to one or more persons, the dictionary form of the verb is used.

AFFIRMATIVE IMPERATIVE	NEGATIVE IMPERATIVE
Answer the phone.	*Don't answer* the phone.
Clean your room.	*Don't clean* your room.
Speak softly.	*Don't speak* softly.

2. "WE" COMMAND — When an order is given to oneself as well as to others, the phrase "let's" (a contraction of *let us*) is used + the dictionary form of the verb.

AFFIRMATIVE IMPERATIVE	NEGATIVE IMPERATIVE
Let's leave.	*Let's not leave.*
Let's go to the movies.	*Let's not go* to the movies.

The absence of the pronoun in the sentence is a good indication that you are dealing with an imperative and not a present tense.

You answer the phone.
|_____|
   present

Answer the phone.
 |
imperative

IN SPANISH

As in English, there are affirmative and negative commands.

————————————— **"You" command** —————————————

There are many forms of the "you" command to distinguish familiar and formal, as well as affirmative and negative.

1. **"Tú" command** — When an order is given to a person to whom you say **tú**.

The regular affirmative **tú** command has the same form as the 3rd person singular of the present indicative tense. There are also several irregular forms that you will have to learn individually. The negative **tú** command has the same form as the 2nd person singular of the present subjunctive.

Affirmative imperative	**Negative imperative**
Habla.	**No hables.**
present indicative	present subjunctive
3rd pers. sing.	2nd pers. sing.
Speak.	*Don't speak.*
Ven aquí.	**No vengas aquí.**
irregular form	present subjunctive
	2nd pers. sing.
Come here.	*Don't come here.*

2. **"Vosotros" command** — When an order is given to two or more persons to whom you say **tú** individually. The **vosotros** command is a familiar plural command and is used only in Spain.

The affirmative **vosotros** command is formed by dropping the -**r** from the infinitive ending and replacing it with the letter -**d**. The negative **vosotros** command has the same form as the 2nd person plural of the present subjunctive.

Affirmative imperative	**Negative imperative**
Venid aquí.	**No vengáis aquí.**
infinitive **venir** *(to come)*	present subjunctive
-**r** → -**d**	2nd per. pl.
Come here.	*Don't come here.*
Hablad.	**No habláis.**
infinitive **hablar** *(to speak)*	present subjunctive
-**r** → -**d**	2nd pers. pl.
Speak.	*Don't speak.*

40

50

60

70

3. "Usted" COMMAND — When an order is given to a person to whom you say **usted**.

Both the affirmative and negative **usted** commands have the same form as the 3rd person singular of the present subjunctive.

80

AFFIRMATIVE IMPERATIVE	NEGATIVE IMPERATIVE
Hable.	**No hable.**
|	|
present subjunctive	present subjunctive
3rd pers. sing.	3rd pers. sing.
Speak.	*Don't speak.*
Venga aquí.	**No venga aquí.**
|	|
present subjunctive	present subjunctive
3rd pers. sing.	3rd pers. sing.
Come here.	*Don't come here.*

90

4. "Ustedes" COMMAND — In Spain: When an order is given to two or more persons to whom you say **usted** individually. In Latin America: When an order is given to two or more persons to whom you say **tú** or **usted** individually.

Both the affirmative and negative **ustedes** commands have the same form as the 3rd person plural of the present subjunctive.

100

AFFIRMATIVE IMPERATIVE	NEGATIVE IMPERATIVE
Hablen.	**No hablen.**
|	|
present subjunctive	present subjunctive
3rd pers. pl.	3rd pers. pl.
Speak.	*Don't speak.*
Vengan aquí.	**No vengan aquí.**
|	|
present subjunctive	present subjunctive
3rd pers. pl.	3rd pers. pl.
Come here.	*Don't come here.*

──────────────── "WE" COMMAND ────────────────

110

When an order is given to oneself as well as to others.

The affirmative and negative **nosotros** commands have the same form as the 1st person plural of the present subjunctive.

AFFIRMATIVE IMPERATIVE	NEGATIVE IMPERATIVE
Hablemos.	**No hablemos.**
|	|
present subjunctive	present subjunctive
1st pers. pl.	1st pers. pl.
Let's talk.	*Let's not talk.*

120

Salgamos.	No salgamos.
present subjunctive	present subjunctive
1ª pers. pl.	1ª pers. pl.
Let's leave.	*Let's not leave.*

Notice that the English phrase *let's* does not translate into Spanish; the command ending is the equivalent of *let's*.

──────────── SUMMARY ────────────

Here is a chart you can use as a reference for choosing the proper form of the Spanish command.

130

COMMAND FORMS		
	AFFIRMATIVE	**NEGATIVE**
tú *you*	present **indicative** 3ʳᵈ pers. sing.	present **subjunctive** 2ⁿᵈ pers. sing.
vosotros *you*	infinitive -r → -d	present **subjunctive** 2ⁿᵈ pers. pl.
usted *you*	present **subjunctive** 3ʳᵈ pers. sing.	present **subjunctive** 3ʳᵈ pers. sing.
ustedes *you*	present **subjunctive** 3ʳᵈ pers. pl.	present **subjunctive** 3ʳᵈ pers. pl.
nosotros *we*	present **subjunctive** 1ª pers. pl.	present **subjunctive** 1ª pers. pl.

140

— *REVIEW* —

A. Change the sentences below to an affirmative command.

1. You must study for the exam.

_____

2. We go to the movies every weekend.

_____

3. You should eat more fruit and vegetables.

_____

B. Change the sentences below to a negative command.

1. You shouldn't sleep in class.

_____

2. You must not work so much.

_____

3. We are not eating out tonight.

_____

WHAT ARE THE PERFECT TENSES?

The **PERFECT TENSES** are compound verbs made up of the
auxiliary verb *to have* + the past participle of
the main verb (see *What is a Participle?*, p. 63).

> I *have* not *seen* him.
> ⎮ ⎮
> auxiliary   past participle
> verb   of *to see*

> They *had* already *gone.*
> ⎮ ⎮
> auxiliary   past participle
> verb   of *to go*

IN ENGLISH───────────────────────

There are four perfect tenses formed with the auxiliary
verb *to have* + the past participle of the main verb. The
name of each perfect tense is based on the tense used for
the auxiliary verb *to have.*

1. **PERFECT** — *to have* in the present tense + the past participle of the main verb (see *What is the Present Tense?*,
   p. 58).

> I *have eaten.*
> ⎮ ⎮
> present   past participle
>   of *to eat*

> The boys *have washed* the car.
> ⎮ ⎮
> present   past participle
>   of *to wash*

2. **PLUPERFECT** — *to have* in the simple past (past definite) +
   the past participle of the main verb (see *What is the Past
   Tense?*, p. 60).

> I *had eaten* before six.
> ⎮ ⎮
> simple past participle
> past   of *to eat*

> The boys *had washed* the car before the storm.
> ⎮ ⎮
> simple   past participle
> past   of *to wash*

3. **FUTURE PERFECT** — *to have* in the future tense + the past participle of the main verb (see *What is the Future Tense?*, p. 83).

> I *shall have eaten* by six.
>   └──┬──┘ |
>   future   past participle
>   of *to eat*

> The boys *will have washed* the car by Thursday.
>   └──┬──┘ |
>   future   past participle
>   of *to wash*

4. **CONDITIONAL PERFECT** — *to have* in the conditional + the past participle of the main verb (see *What is the Conditional?*, p. 86).

> I *would have eaten* if I had had the time.
>   └──┬──┘ |
> conditional past participle
>   of *to eat*

> John *would have washed* the car if he had been here.
>   └──┬──┘ |
> conditional past participle
>   of *to wash*

IN SPANISH

The perfect tenses are made up of a form of the auxiliary verb **haber** *(to have)* + the past participle of the main verb. In Spanish there are several perfect tenses: four perfect tenses in the indicative mood (see *What is Meant by Mood?*, p. 69) and two in the subjunctive (see *What is the Subjunctive?*, p. 71). As in English, the name of the tense is based on the tense of the auxiliary verb **haber**.

We are listing the various perfect tenses here so that you can see the pattern that they follow. The perfect tenses are not always used in the same way in Spanish as in English. Consult your Spanish textbook in order to learn to use them properly.

──── SPANISH PERFECT TENSES IN THE INDICATIVE MOOD ────

1. **PERFECT** (PERFECTO) — **haber** in the present tense + the past participle of the main verb. Generally the Spanish perfect is used in the same way as the perfect in English.

> **He comido.**
> *I have eaten.*

> Los chicos **han lavado** el coche.
> *The boys **have washed** the car.*

2. **PLUPERFECT** (PLUSCUAMPERFECTO) — **haber** in the imperfect + the past participle of the main verb. The pluperfect tense is used to express an action completed in the past before some other past action or event. Generally, the Spanish pluperfect is used the same way as the pluperfect in English.

> **Había comido** antes de las seis.
> *I had eaten before six.*

> Los chicos **habían lavado** el coche antes de la tempestad.
> *The boys had washed the car before the storm.*

3. **FUTURE PERFECT** (FUTURO PERFECTO) — **haber** in the future + the past participle of the main verb. Generally, the Spanish future perfect is used in the same way as the future perfect in English.

> **Habré comido** para las seis.
> *I shall have eaten by six.*

> Los chicos **habrán lavado** el coche para el jueves.
> *The boys will have washed the car by Thursday.*

4. **CONDITIONAL PERFECT** (CONDICIONAL PERFECTO) — **haber** in the conditional + the past participle of the main verb.

> **Habría comido** si hubiera tenido el tiempo.
> *I would have eaten if I had had the time.*

> Los chicos **habrían lavado** el coche si hubieran estado aquí.
> *The boys would have washed the car if they had been here.*

———— SPANISH PERFECT TENSES IN THE SUBJUNCTIVE MOOD ————

1. **PERFECT SUBJUNCTIVE** (PERFECTO DEL SUBJUNTIVO) — **haber** in the present subjunctive + the past participle of the main verb. This tense is really just a perfect used when a subjunctive is required.

> *He hopes that **they have arrived**.*
> requires that   perfect subjunctive → **hayan llegado**
> the following
> verb be in the subjunctive

2. **PLUPERFECT SUBJUNCTIVE** (PLUSCUAMPERFECTO DEL SUBJUNTIVO) — **haber** in the imperfect subjunctive + the past participle of the main verb.

> *He hoped that **they had arrived**.*
> requires that   pluperfect subjunctive → **hubieran llegado**
> the following
> verb be in the subjunctive

80

90

100

110

120

— *REVIEW* —

Underline the verbs in a perfect tense.

- Indicate the tense of the verb in italics: perfect (P), pluperfect (PP), future perfect (FP) or conditional perfect (CP).

1. We *had* already *gone* when Teresa arrived.	P	PP	FP	CP
2. Barbara *hasn't left* yet.	P	PP	FP	CP
3. I *shall have graduated* by next summer.	P	PP	FP	CP
4. We *would have studied* more	P	PP	FP	CP
if we *had remembered* the exam.	P	PP	FP	CP
5. *Have* you *seen* my new car?	P	PP	FP	CP

25

WHAT IS THE FUTURE TENSE?

> The FUTURE TENSE indicates that an action will take
> place some time in the future.

> I *shall return* the book as soon as I've read it.
> └──┬──┘
> future

IN ENGLISH

The future tense is formed with the auxiliary *will* or *shall*
+ the dictionary form of the main verb. In conversation
shall and *will* are often shortened to *'ll*.

> Paul and Mary *will do* their homework tomorrow.
> *I'll leave* tonight.

IN SPANISH

You do not need an auxiliary to show that an action will
take place. The future tense is indicated by a simple tense.
   Regular verbs use the infinitive as a stem for the future
tense.

INFINITIVE	STEM	
visitar	visitar-	*to visit*
comer	comer-	*to eat*
vivir	vivir-	*to live*

Irregular verbs have irregular future stems that you will
have to memorize individually. Your textbook will list
irregular future verb stems and give you the endings to be
added in order to form the future tense.

─── SUBSTITUTE FOR THE FUTURE TENSE ───

In English and in Spanish an action that will occur some
time in the future can also be expressed without using the
future tense itself, but with a construction that implies the
future.

IN ENGLISH

The immediate future is expressed with the verb *to go* in
the present continuous tense + the infinitive of the main
verb: *I am going to travel, she is going to dance.*

[handwritten margin notes: 1 ... 10 OVER SIMPLE form in English has NO Future Tense but 20 modality expressed with will/shall as modals! 30]

40

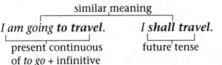

similar meaning

I am going to travel.   *I shall travel.*
present continuous   future tense
of *to go* + infinitive

IN SPANISH

The same construction exists in Spanish; it is formed with the verb **ir** *(to go)* in the present tense + **a** + the infinitive of the main verb: **voy a viajar** *(I'm going to travel)*, **ella va a bailar** *(she's going to dance)*.

Look at the difference between the forms of the two constructions.

50

similar meaning

Voy a estudiar.   **Estudiaré.**
present of **ir** +   future tense
a + infinitive

I am going to study.   *I shall study.*
present continuous   future tense
of *to go* + infinitive

CAREFUL — Note that the "a" has no English equivalent; it must appear in the Spanish sentence, however.

60

─────────── **FUTURE OF PROBABILITY** ───────────

In addition to expressing an action that will take place in the future, the future tense in Spanish can be used to express a probable fact, what the speaker feels is probably true. This is called the **FUTURE OF PROBABILITY**.

IN ENGLISH

The idea of probability is expressed with words such as *must, probably, wonder.*

70

My keys *must* be around here.
My keys are *probably* around here.
I *wonder* if my keys are around here.

IN SPANISH

It is not necessary to use the words *must, probably,* or *wonder* to express probable facts; the main verb is simply put into the future tense.

I wonder what time it is.
present tense   main verb → present tense

80

¿Qué hora **será**?
main verb future tense

It's probably 4:00.
|
main verb *is* → present tense
Serán las cuatro.
|
main verb → future tense

*I can't find my book. John **must have** it.*
|
main verb → infinitive
No puedo encontrar mi libro. Juan lo **tendrá**.
|
main verb → future tense

90

— *REVIEW* —

Circle the verbs in the following sentences.
- On the line provided, write the dictionary form of the English verb you would put in the future tense in Spanish.

DICTIONARY FORM

1. The students will study for the exam.   _____

2. I'll clean my room later.   _____

3. Shall we leave?   _____

4. I won't finish until tomorrow.   _____

5. Will she be here by 9:00?   _____

CHAPTER

26

WHAT IS THE CONDITIONAL?

The **CONDITIONAL** forms of a verb get their name because they are primarily used in sentences that imply a condition.

If I were offered the job, I *would take* it.

      condition   conditional form of the verb

The conditional has a present and past tense called the conditional (present) and the conditional perfect (past).

CONDITIONAL (PRESENT)

IN ENGLISH

The conditional is a compound tense made up of the auxiliary **would** + the dictionary form of the main verb: I *would eat.*

The conditional is used in the following ways:

1. as a polite form with *like* and in polite requests

> I *would like* to eat.
> More polite than "I want to eat."

> *Would* you please close the door.
> "Please close the door" is softened by the use of *would.*

2. in the result clause of a hypothetical statement

A **HYPOTHETICAL STATEMENT** includes a condition that does not exist at the present time, but could possibly become a reality one day.

      condition   result clause

If Paul had money, he *would buy* a house.

subject verb   subject verb in the conditional

The above statement is hypothetical because Paul does not have money at the present time; but there is the possibility that he will have money someday and, therefore, be able to buy a house.

A **CLAUSE** is a part of a sentence composed of a group of words containing a subject and a verb. In a hypothetical statement there are two types of clauses: the *if* clause and the result clause.

- **IF CLAUSE** — expresses the condition which must be met. In the above example: "If Paul had money...."
- **RESULT CLAUSE** — expresses the result if the condition is met. In the above example: "he would buy a house."

3. in an indirect statement to express a future-in-the-past

An **INDIRECT STATEMENT** repeats, or reports, but does not quote, someone's words, as opposed to a **DIRECT STATEMENT** which is a word-for-word quotation of what someone said. In written form a direct statement is always between quotation marks.

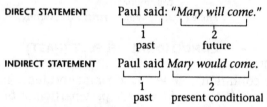

In the direct statement, action 2 is merely a quotation in the future tense. In an indirect statement, action 2 *(Mary would come)* is called a **FUTURE-IN-THE-PAST** because it takes place after another action in the past *(Paul said)*.

IN SPANISH

Unlike English, you do not need an auxiliary verb to indicate the conditional. It is a simple tense formed with the future stem (see p. 83) + the endings of the imperfect tense for -**er** and -**ir** verbs (see your textbook).

FUTURE STEM	CONDITIONAL	
hablar-	hablaría	*I would speak*
comer-	comería	*I would eat*
vivir-	viviría	*I would live*
pondr-	pondría	*I would put*
har-	haría	*I would do*

The conditional is used in the same ways as in English:

1. as a polite form or in polite requests

Querría un vaso de agua.
conditional
I would like a glass of water.

¿Podría Ud. cerrar la puerta, por favor?
conditional
Would you close the door, please?

2. in the result clause of a hypothetical statement

Si tuviera mucho dinero, **compraría** una casa grande.
|
conditional

*If I had a lot of money, **I would buy** a big house.*

3. in an indirect statement to express a future-in-the-past

Dijo que **vendría.**
|
conditional

*He said (that) **he would come.***

Sabía que **llovería** esta noche.
|
conditional

*I knew (that) **it would rain** this evening.*

———— CONDITIONAL PERFECT (PAST) ————

IN ENGLISH

The conditional perfect is a compound tense made up of the auxiliary ***would have*** + past participle of the main verb: *I would have eaten, he would have come.*

The conditional perfect is only used in the result clause of contrary-to-fact statements.

A statement is **CONTRARY-TO-FACT** when a condition was not met in the past and therefore the result was not accomplished.

      if clause   result clause

If I had had money, I *would have bought* a new house.

The statement above is contrary-to-fact because the person speaking didn't have money in the past and therefore did not buy a new house.

He *would have spoken* if he had known the truth.
Contrary-to-fact: He did not speak
because he didn't know the truth.

If you had called us, we *would have come.*
Contrary-to-fact: We did not come
because you didn't call us.

IN SPANISH

The conditional perfect is a compound tense made up of the auxiliary verb **haber** *(to have)* in the conditional tense + the past participle of the main verb: **habría hablado** *(I would have spoken)*. As in English, statements using the conditional perfect are contrary-to-fact.

Si hubieran estudiado más, **habrían recibido** mejores notas.
conditional perfect
*If they had studied more, **they would have received** better grades.*

SEQUENCE OF TENSES

Let us look at examples of hypothetical and contrary-to-fact statements so that you learn to use the appropriate tense in each clause. [130]

Hypothetical and contrary-to-fact statements are easy to recognize because they are made up of two clauses:

- the IF CLAUSE (the clause that starts with *if, si* in Spanish)
- the RESULT CLAUSE

The sequence of tenses is sometimes the same in both English and Spanish. If you have difficulty recognizing tenses, just apply these three rules.

"IF" CLAUSE → PRESENT   RESULT CLAUSE → FUTURE [140]

---

*If I **have** time, I **shall go** to the party.*
present   future
Si **tengo** tiempo, **iré** a la fiesta.
present   future

"IF" CLAUSE → PAST (English)   RESULT CLAUSE → CONDITIONAL
IMPERFECT SUBJUNCTIVE (Spanish)

---

*If I **had** more time, I **would go** to the party.* [150]
past   conditional
Si **tuviera** más tiempo, **iría** a la fiesta.
imperfect   conditional
subjunctive

"IF" CLAUSE → PLUPERFECT (English)   RESULT CLAUSE → CONDITIONAL PERFECT
PLUPERFECT SUBJUNCTIVE (Spanish)

---

*If I **had had** more time, I **would have gone** to the party.*
pluperfect   conditional perfect [160]
Si **hubiera tenido** más tiempo, **habría ido** a la fiesta.
pluperfect   conditional perfect
subjunctive

CAREFUL — In English and in Spanish, the *if clause* can come before or after the result clause. The tense of a clause remains the same regardless of the order of the clauses.

I would have gone to the party, if I had had more time.
conditional perfect   pluperfect

Habría ido a la fiesta, si **hubiera tenido** más tiempo.
conditional perfect   pluperfect
                             subjunctive

— R E V I E W —

Write the tense you would use in Spanish for each of the italicized verbs below: present (P), preterite (PT), future (F), conditional (C), conditional perfect (CP), imperfect subjunctive (IS), or the pluperfect subjunctive (PS).

1. I *know* the children *will enjoy* that movie.

   _____   _____

2. We *would go* to Spain if we *had* the money.

   _____   _____

3. I *would like* some more meat, please.

   _____

4. If it *rains*, they *won't have* the picnic.

   _____   _____

5. My parents *wrote* that they *would come* in July.

   _____   _____

6. If I *had known* you were coming, I *wouldn't have left*.

   _____   _____

WHAT IS MEANT BY ACTIVE
AND PASSIVE VOICE?

Voice in the grammatical sense refers to the relationship
between the verb and its subject. There are two voices,
the ACTIVE VOICE and the PASSIVE VOICE.

ACTIVE VOICE — A sentence is said to be in the active voice
when the subject is the performer of the action of the
verb. In this instance, the verb is called an ACTIVE VERB.

The teacher prepares the exam.
  | | |
  S   V   DO

Paul ate an apple.
  | | |
  S   V   DO

Lightning has struck the tree.
    | └──┬──┘ |
    S   V   DO

In these examples the subject (S) performs the action of
the verb (V) and the direct object (DO) is the receiver of
the action (see *What is a Subject?*, p. 23 and *What are
Objects?*, p. 124).

PASSIVE VOICE — A sentence is said to be in the passive
voice when the subject is the receiver of the action of the
verb. In this instance, the verb is called a PASSIVE VERB.

The exam is prepared by the teacher.
  | └──┬───┘ |
  S   V   agent

The apple was eaten by Paul.
  | └──┬──┘ |
  S   V   agent

The tree has been struck by lightning.
  | └────┬──────┘ |
  S   V   agent

In these examples, the subject is the receiver of the
action of the verb. The performer of the action, if it is
mentioned, is introduced by the word "by" and is called
the AGENT.

IN ENGLISH —————————————————————————————

The passive voice is expressed by the verb *to be* conjugated
in the appropriate tense + the past participle of the main

verb (see *What is a Participle?*, p. 63). The tense of the passive sentence is indicated by the tense of the verb *to be*.

The exam *is prepared* by the teacher.
present

The exam *was prepared* by the teacher.
past

The exam *will be prepared* by the teacher.
future

IN SPANISH

As in English, a passive verb can be expressed by the auxiliary verb **ser** *(to be)* conjugated in the appropriate tense + the past participle of the main verb. The tense of the passive sentence is indicated by the tense of the verb **ser**.

El examen **es** preparado por el profesor.
present
The exam is prepared by the teacher.

El examen **fue** preparado por el profesor.
past
The exam has been (was) prepared by the teacher.

El examen **será** preparado por el profesor.
future
The exam will be prepared by the teacher.

In the passive voice formed with **ser** all past participles agree in gender and number with the subject.

Esas **cartas** fueron **escritas** por el profesor.
fem. pl.   fem. pl.
Those letters were written by the teacher.

———— MAKING AN ACTIVE SENTENCE PASSIVE ————

The steps to change an active sentence to a passive sentence are the same in English and in Spanish.

1. The direct object of the active sentence is made the subject of the passive sentence.

ACTIVE   The teacher prepares *the exam.*
direct object

PASSIVE   *The exam* is prepared by the teacher.
subject

2. The tense of the verb of the active sentence is reflected   80
   in the tense of the verb *to be* in the passive sentence.

   ACTIVE   The teacher *prepares* the exam.
                                  |
                                present
   PASSIVE   The exam *is* prepared by the teacher.
                        |
                      present

   ACTIVE   The teacher *prepared* the exam.
                                   |
                                 past
   PASSIVE   The exam *was* prepared by the teacher.   90
                        |
                      past

   ACTIVE   The teacher *will* prepare the exam.
                             |
                           future
   PASSIVE   The exam *will be* prepared by the teacher.
                        |___|
                        future

3. The subject of the active sentence is made the agent of
   the passive sentence introduced with *by*.

   ACTIVE   *The teacher* prepares the exam.
                     |
                   subject   100
   PASSIVE   The exam is prepared *by the teacher*.
                                         |
                                       agent

──────── **AVOIDING THE PASSIVE VOICE IN SPANISH** ────────

Although Spanish has a passive voice, whenever possible
Spanish speakers try to avoid it by replacing it with an
active construction. This is particularly true for general
statements when we don't know who is doing the action.

> English *is spoken* in many countries.   110
> We don't know who is speaking.

> The New York Times *is sold* here.
> We don't know who is selling.

There are two ways a passive sentence can be avoided in
Spanish.

1. using the **se** construction — The word **se** corresponds
   to the English indefinite pronoun *one* used in a general
   sense as in the sentence "*One* should eat when *one* is
   hungry." Spanish often makes *one* the subject of an   120
   active sentence, even in cases where English speakers
   would never use such a construction.

English is spoken in many countries.
        └──┬──┘
     "one speaks"
Se habla inglés en muchos países.

The New York Times is sold here.
            └──┬──┘
         "one sells"
Se vende el New York Times aquí.

2. using the 3rd person plural of the verb — The main verb of the sentence is changed from the English passive voice to the equivalent Spanish 3rd person plural. The subject of the English sentence becomes the direct object in the Spanish sentence. The "they" corresponds to a general subject, such as *"They say Mexico is very interesting."*

English is spoken in many countries.
         │   │
     subject + passive verb
"they speak English"
└─────────┬─────────┘
3rd pers. pl. + active verb + DO
Hablan inglés en muchos países.

The New York Times is sold here.
         │   │
     subject + passive verb
"they sell the New York Times"
└─────────────┬─────────────┘
3rd pers. pl. + active verb + DO
Venden el New York Times aquí.

CAREFUL — Make sure you distinguish between the auxiliary **haber** *(to have)* + the past participle used to form a past tense in the active voice (see *What are the Perfect Tenses?*, p. 79) and **ser** *(to be)* + the past participle used to form a passive sentence. For example, **ha cerrado** is a past tense of the verb **cerrar** *(to close)* in the active voice and **fue cerrado** is a past tense in the passive voice. As you can see in the following examples, the same changes occur in English.

ACTIVE   *The teacher **has** prepared the exam.*

▼   auxiliary *to have* → past (perfect)   160

PASSIVE   *The exam **was** prepared by the teacher.*

            auxiliary *to be* → past

ACTIVE   El profesor **ha** escrito el examen.

▼   auxiliary **haber** *(to have)* → past (perfect)

PASSIVE   El examen **fue** escrito por el profesor.

            auxiliary **ser** *(to be)* → past

— REVIEW —

Underline the subjects in the sentences below.

- Circle the performer of the action.
- Identify each sentence as active (Ac) or passive (Pa).
- Identify the tense of the verb: past (PP), present (P), future (F).

1. The cow jumped over the moon.   Ac   Pa   PP P F

2. The bill was paid by Bob's parents.   Ac   Pa   PP P F

3. The bank transfers the money.   Ac   Pa   PP P F

4. Everyone will be going away
during August.   Ac   Pa   PP P F

5. The spring break will be enjoyed
by all.   Ac   Pa   PP P F

WHAT IS AN ADJECTIVE?

1   An **ADJECTIVE** is a word that describes a noun or a pronoun.
There are different types of adjectives; they
are classified according to the way
they describe a noun or pronoun.

DESCRIPTIVE ADJECTIVE — A descriptive adjective indicates a quality; it tells what kind of noun it is (see p. 97).
>   She read an *interesting* book.
>   He has *brown* eyes.

10   **POSSESSIVE ADJECTIVE**— A possessive adjective shows possession; it tells whose noun it is (see p. 100).
>   *His* book is lost.
>   *Our* parents are away.

INTERROGATIVE ADJECTIVE — An interrogative adjective asks a question about a noun (see p. 107).
>   *What* book is lost?
>   *Which* book did you read?

DEMONSTRATIVE ADJECTIVE — A demonstrative adjective points out a noun (see p. 110).
20
>   *This* teacher is excellent.
>   *That* question is very appropriate.

IN ENGLISH ───────────────────────────
English adjectives usually do not change their form, regardless of the noun or pronouns described.

IN SPANISH ───────────────────────────
The principal difference between English and Spanish adjectives is that while in English adjectives do not change their form, in Spanish adjectives change in order
30   to agree in gender and number with the noun or pronoun they modify.

WHAT IS A DESCRIPTIVE ADJECTIVE?

A DESCRIPTIVE ADJECTIVE is a word that indicates a quality of a   1
noun or pronoun. As the name implies, it
describes the noun or pronoun.

The book is *interesting.*
    | |
  noun   descriptive
  described adjective

IN ENGLISH ───────────────────────────────
A descriptive adjective does not change form, regardless of
the noun or pronoun it modifies.

    10

The students are *intelligent.*
She is an *intelligent* person.

The form of the adjective *intelligent* remains the same
although the persons described are different in number
(*students* is plural and *person* is singular).

Descriptive adjectives are divided into two groups
depending on how they are connected to the noun they
modify.

1. A PREDICATE ADJECTIVE is connected to the noun it
   describes, always the subject of the sentence, by LINKING   20
   VERBS such as *to be, to feel, to look.*

   The children are *good.*
      | | |
     noun   linking predicate
     described verb   adjective

   The house looks *small.*
      | | |
     noun   linking predicate
     described verb   adjective

2. An ATTRIBUTIVE ADJECTIVE is connected directly to the
   noun it describes and always precedes it.   30

   The *good* children were praised.
     | |
   attributive noun
   adjective   described

   The family lives in a *small* house.
              | |
         attributive noun
         adjective   described

IN SPANISH

As in English, descriptive adjectives can be identified as predicate or attribute adjectives according to the way they are connected to the noun they describe.

Spanish descriptive adjectives differ in two important ways from English descriptive adjectives.

1. While English descriptive adjectives never change form, all Spanish descriptive adjectives, predicate and attributive, change form in order to agree in gender and number with the noun or pronoun they modify.

Most adjectives change the final "-o" of the masculine singular form to "-a" to make the feminine form and add "-s" to the masculine singular or the feminine singular form to make it plural.

the red car	el coche **rojo**
	masc. masc.
	sing. sing.

the red table	la mesa **roja**
	fem. fem. (final -o → -a)
	sing. sing.

the red cars	los coches **rojos**
	masc. masc. (rojo + -s)
	pl. pl.

the red tables	las mesas **rojas**
	fem. fem. (roja + -s)
	pl. pl.

2. While English descriptive adjectives always come before the noun they modify, most, but not all, Spanish descriptive adjectives come after the noun they modify.

> Ella lee un libro **interesante**.
> *She is reading an **interesting** book.*

However, some common Spanish descriptive adjectives come before the noun they modify.

> Juan es un **buen** chico.
> *John is a **good** boy.*

Your textbook will tell you, and you will have to learn, which Spanish descriptive adjectives precede and which follow the noun they modify.

———————— NOUNS USED AS ADJECTIVES ———————— 80

Occasionally, a noun is used as an adjective; that is, it is used to modify another noun.

IN ENGLISH

When a noun is used to describe another noun, the structure is as follows: the describing noun (adjective) + the noun described.

    Spanish is easy.   The *Spanish* class is crowded.
      | | |
     noun   adjective noun described

90

    Chemistry is difficult.   The *chemistry* books are expensive.
       | | |
     noun   adjective noun described

IN SPANISH

It is important that you recognize a noun acting as an adjective because it remains a noun and does not change form. In the examples below, you will see that the noun described and the noun acting as an adjective have different genders and numbers.

When a noun is used as an adjective, the structure is as follows: the noun described + **de** *(of)* + the describing noun (adjective) without an article. 100

    the Spanish class   la **clase** de **español**
      | | | |
  el **español** la **clase**   fem. sing. masc. sing.
                          noun   noun/adjective
                          described

    the chemistry books   los **libros** de **química**
      | | | |
  la **química** los **libros**   masc. pl.   fem. sing.
                          noun   noun/adjective
                          described

— REVIEW —

Circle the adjectives in the sentences below.
- Draw an arrow from the adjective you circled to the noun or pronoun described.

1. The young man was reading a Spanish newspaper.

2. She looked pretty in her new red dress.

3. It is interesting.

4. The old piano could still produce good music.

5. Paul was tired after his long walk.

CHAPTER

30

WHAT IS A POSSESSIVE ADJECTIVE?

A POSSESSIVE ADJECTIVE is a word that describes a noun
by showing who possesses that noun.

> Whose house is that? It's *my* house.
>> *My* shows who possesses the noun *house*. The
>> possessor is "me." The object possessed is *house*.

IN ENGLISH ————————————————————————

Like subject pronouns, possessive adjectives are identified
according to the person they represent (see p. 27).

SINGULAR POSSESSOR
1ST PERSON		my
2ND PERSON		your
	MASCULINE	his
3RD PERSON	FEMININE	her
	NEUTER	its

PLURAL POSSESSOR
1ST PERSON	our
2ND PERSON	your
3RD PERSON	their

A possessive adjective changes to identify the possessor,
regardless of the objects possessed.

> Is that John's house? Yes, it is *his* house.
> Is that Mary's house? Yes, it is *her* house.
>> Although the object possessed is the same *(house)*, different
>> possessive adjectives *(his* and *her)* are used because the pos-
>> sessors are different *(John* and *Mary).*

> Is that John's house? Yes, it is *his* house.
> Are those John's keys? Yes, they are *his* keys.
>> Although the objects possessed are different *(house* and
>> *keys)*, the same possessive adjective *(his)* is used because the
>> possessor is the same *(John).*

IN SPANISH ————————————————————————

Like English, a Spanish possessive adjective changes to
identify the possessor, but unlike English it also agrees,
like all Spanish adjectives, in gender and number with the
noun possessed.

For example, in the phrase "nuestro hermano" *(our brother)* the possessor *(our)* is indicated by the first letters of the 1ˢᵗ person plural possessive adjective **nuestr-**, and the gender and number of the noun possessed, **hermano** *(brother)*, which is masculine singular, is reflected in the masculine singular ending **-o**. Let us see what happens when we change *our brother* to *our sister*.

> *We love **our sister**.*
> Queremos a **nuestra hermana**.
> ⌐─┬─┐│
>   │ fem. sing. ending
> 1ˢᵗ pers. pl.
> possessor

> The first letters **nuestr-** remain the same because the possessor is still the 1ˢᵗ person plural, but the ending changes to **-a** to agree with **hermana** *(sister)* which is feminine singular.

Spanish has two sets of possessive adjectives: the STRESSED POSSESSIVE ADJECTIVES and the UNSTRESSED POSSESSIVE ADJECTIVES. The short, unstressed forms are the most common and will be considered first.

──────────── UNSTRESSED POSSESSIVE ADJECTIVES ────────────

──────── MY, YOUR (TÚ, USTED, USTEDES FORMS), HIS, HER, THEIR ────────

In Spanish, each of the above possessive adjectives has two forms, a singular and a plural form. You will choose the one which agrees with the number of the noun possessed.

To choose the correct form of the possessive adjective:

1. Indicate the possessor. This is shown by the first two letters of the possessive adjective.

my	**mi**
your [tú form]	**tu**

his	
her	
your [usted form]	**su**
their	
your [ustedes form]	

2. Choose the ending according to the number of the noun possessed.

   - noun possessed is singular → the form of the possessive adjective does not change

Ana lee **mi** libro.   *Ana reads **my** book.*
|
noun possessed singular
Ana lee **tu** libro.   *Ana reads **your** book.*
Ana lee **su** libro.   *Ana reads **her** (**his, your, their**) book.*

- noun possessed is plural → add -s to the possessive adjective

Ana lee **mis** libros.   *Ana reads **my** books.*
|
noun possessed plural
Ana lee **tus** libros.   *Ana reads **your** books.*
Ana lee **sus** libros.   *Ana reads **her** (**his, your, their**) books.*

Because the possessive adjective **su** has many meanings, Spanish speakers often replace it with the phrase: noun + **de** + pronoun.

el libro **de él**	*his book*
el libro **de ella**	*her book*
su libro ⎰ el libro **de Ud.**	*your book*
⎱ el libro **de ellos**	*their book*
el libro **de ellas**	*their book*
el libro **de Uds.**	*your book*

You will have to rely on context to establish the English equivalent of the possessive adjectives **su** and **sus**.

Let us apply the above steps to examples:

*I am looking for **my** car.*
    1. POSSESSOR: *my* → 1ª pers. sing. → **mi**
    2. NUMBER NOUN POSSESSED: **coche** *(car)* → singular
    3. SELECTION: **mi**
Busco **mi** coche.

*I am looking for **my** keys.*
    1. POSSESSOR: *my* → 1ª pers. sing. → **mi-**
    2. NUMBER NOUN POSSESSED: **llaves** *(keys)* → plural
    3. SELECTION: **mi- + -s**
Busco **mis** llaves.

─────────────── OUR, YOUR (VOSOTROS FORM) ───────────────

In Spanish, the two possessive adjectives above have four forms, a masculine singular, a feminine singular, a masculine plural, and a feminine plural. You will choose the one which agrees with the gender and number of the noun possessed.

To choose the correct form of the possessive adjective:
1. Indicate the possessor. This is shown by the first letters of the possessive adjective.

our	**nuestr-**
your [vosotros form]	**vuestr-**

2. Choose the ending according to the gender and number of the noun possessed.

- noun possessed is masculine singular → add -o

  Ana lee **nuestro** libro. *Ana reads our book.*

  noun possessed masc. sing.

  Ana lee **vuestro** libro. *Ana reads your book.*

- noun possessed is feminine singular → add -a

  Ana lee **nuestra** revista. *Ana reads our magazine.*

  noun possessed fem. sing.

  Ana lee **vuestra** revista. *Ana reads your magazine.*

- noun possessed is masculine plural → add -os

  Ana lee **nuestros** libros. *Ana reads our books.*

  noun possessed masc. pl.

  Ana lee **vuestros** libros. *Ana reads your books.*

- noun possessed is feminine plural → add -as

  Ana lee **nuestras** revistas. *Ana reads our magazines.*

  noun possessed fem. pl.

  Ana lee **vuestras** revistas. *Ana reads your magazines.*

Let us apply the above steps to examples:

We are looking for our car.
1. POSSESSOR: *our* → 1ˢᵗ pers. pl. → **nuestr-**
2. GENDER & NUMBER NOUN POSSESSED: **coche** *(car)* → masc. sing.
3. SELECTION: **nuestr-** + **-o**

Buscamos **nuestro** coche.

We are looking for our keys.
1. POSSESSOR: *our* → 1ˢᵗ pers. pl. → **nuestr-**
2. GENDER & NUMBER NOUN POSSESSED: **llaves** *(keys)* → fem. pl.
3. SELECTION: **nuestr-** + **-as**

Buscamos **nuestras** llaves.

Notice that unstressed possessive adjectives are placed before the noun they modify.

CAREFUL — Make sure that the ending of possessive adjectives agrees with the noun modified and not with the possessor.

———————— STRESSED POSSESSIVE ADJECTIVES ————————

Spanish also has another set of possessive adjectives called
STRESSED POSSESSIVE ADJECTIVES. They are used to add emphasis to the possessor and correspond to the English "of
mine," "of yours," etc.

> Where is that *dress of mine?*
>
> instead of *my dress*

> Where are those *books of yours?*
>
> instead of *your books*

The use of these stressed forms is more common in
Spanish than in English.

The stressed possessive adjectives have four forms, a masculine singular, a feminine singular, a masculine plural,
and a feminine plural. You will choose the one that agrees
with the gender and number of the noun possessed.

To choose the correct stressed possessive adjective:

1. Indicate the possessor. This is shown by the first letters
   of the possessive adjective.

mine, of mine	**mí-**
your, of yours [tú form]	**tuy-**
his, of his	
her, of hers	**suy-**
your, of yours [usted form]	
our, of ours	**nuestr-**
your, of yours [vosotros form]	**vuestr-**
their, of theirs	
your, of yours [ustedes form]	**suy-**

2. Choose the ending according to the gender and number of the noun possessed.
   - noun possessed is masculine singular → add -o

     > Ana lee un libro **mío.**
     >
     > noun possessed masc. sing.
     >
     > *Ana is reading a book of mine.*

   - noun possessed is feminine singular→ add -a

     > Ana lee una revista **mía.**
     >
     > noun possessed fem. sing.
     >
     > *Ana is reading a magazine of mine.*

170

180

190

200

- noun possessed is masculine plural → add -os

Ana lee unos libros **míos**.
|
noun possessed masc. pl.
Ana is reading some books of mine.

- noun possessed is feminine plural → add -as

Ana lee unas revistas **mías**.
|
noun possessed fem. pl.
Ana is reading some magazines of mine.

Let us apply the above steps to examples:

This car is John's. My car is in the garage.
1. POSSESSOR: *my* → 1ˢᵗ pers. sing. → **mí-**
2. GENDER & NUMBER NOUN POSSESSED: **coche** (*car*) → masc. sing.
3. SELECTION: **mí-** + **-o**

El coche **mío** está en el garaje.

These chairs of yours are very comfortable.
1. POSSESSOR: *of yours* → 2ⁿᵈ pers. sing. → **tuy-**
2. GENDER & NUMBER NOUN POSSESSED: **sillas** (*chairs*) → fem. pl.
3. SELECTION: **tuy-** + **-as**

Estas sillas **tuyas** son muy cómodas.

Notice that stressed possessive adjectives are placed after the noun they modify.

─────────────── **SUMMARY** ───────────────

Here are two charts you can use as a reference.

POSSESSOR	UNSTRESSED POSSESSIVE ADJECTIVES		
	NOUN POSSESSED		
		SINGULAR	PLURAL
my	MASC. FEM.	mi	mis
your [tú form]	MASC. FEM.	tu	tus
his, her, *your* [usted form]	MASC. FEM.	su	sus
our	MASC. FEM.	nuestro nuestra	nuestros nuestras
your [vosotros form]	MASC. FEM.	vuestro vuestra	vuestros vuestras
their, *your* [ustedes form]	MASC. FEM.	su	sus

POSSESSOR		STRESSED POSSESSIVE ADJECTIVES	
		NOUN POSSESSED	
		SINGULAR	PLURAL
my, of mine	MASC.	mío	míos
	FEM.	mía	mías
your [tú form]	MASC.	tuyo	tuyos
	FEM.	tuya	tuyas
his, her, *your* [usted form]	MASC.	suyo	suyos
	FEM.	suya	suyas
our	MASC.	nuestro	nuestros
	FEM.	nuestra	nuestras
your [vosotros form]	MASC.	vuestro	vuestros
	FEM.	vuestra	vuestras
their, *your* [ustedes form]	MASC.	suyo	suyos
	FEM.	suya	suyas

250

260

— REVIEW —

Circle the possessive adjectives in the sentences below.

- Draw an arrow from the possessive adjective to the noun it modifies.
- Circle singular (S) or plural (P) to indicate the ending of the Spanish possessive adjective.
- Using the charts in this section, fill in the Spanish unstressed possessive adjective in the Spanish sentences below.

1. I put my book on the desk.

> NOUN MODIFIED IN SPANISH: masculine   S   P

Puse _____ libro sobre el escritorio.

2. Mary is wearing your (familiar) boots.

> NOUN MODIFIED IN SPANISH: feminine   S   P

María lleva_____ botas.

3. Roberto is looking for his mother.

> NOUN MODIFIED IN SPANISH: feminine   S   P

Roberto busca a _____ madre.

4. Our children are very young.

> NOUN MODIFIED IN SPANISH: masculine   S   P

_____ hijos son muy jóvenes.

31

WHAT IS AN INTERROGATIVE ADJECTIVE?

An **INTERROGATIVE ADJECTIVE** is a word that asks for
information about a noun.   1

> *Which* book do you want?
> |
> asks information about the noun *book*

IN ENGLISH

The words *which* and *what* are called interrogative adjectives when they come in front of a noun and are used to
ask a question about that noun.

> *Which* instructor is teaching the course?   10
> *What* courses are you taking?

IN SPANISH

There are two interrogative adjectives: 1. **qué** which corresponds to the English *which* or *what* and 2. the forms of
cuánto meaning *how much* or *how many*.[1]

1. *which* or *what* + noun → **qué** + noun

   Qué is invariable; that is, it does not change form.

   > ¿**Qué** revista lees?
   > *What magazine are you reading?*   20
   >
   > ¿**Qué** libros quieres?
   > *Which books do you want?*

2. *how much* or *how many* + noun → **cuánto** + noun

   Cuánto changes forms to agree in number and gender
   with the noun it modifies. Therefore, in order to
   choose the correct form of **cuánto**, begin by analyzing
   the noun modified.

   - noun modified is masculine singular → **cuánto**   30

     > ¿**Cuánto** dinero necesitas?
     >
     > Dinero *(money)* is masculine singular, so the word for
     > "how much" must be masculine singular.
     >
     > *How much money do you need?*

---

[1]**Qué** is used in standard Spanish. In certain areas of the Spanish-speaking world **cuál**
and **cuáles** can function as interrogative adjectives: ¿**Cuál** libro quieres? *Which book do
you want?*

- noun modified is feminine singular → **cuánta**

  ¿Cuánta sopa quieres?
  Sopa *(soup)* is feminine singular, so the word for "how much" must be feminine singular.
  How much soup do you want?

- noun modified is masculine plural→ **cuántos**

  ¿Cuántos discos tienes?
  Discos *(CDs)* is masculine plural, so the word for "how many" must be masculine plural.
  How many CDs do you have?

- noun modified is feminine plural → **cuántas**

  ¿Cuántas maletas traes?
  Maletas *(suitcases)* is feminine plural, so the word for "how many" must be feminine plural.
  How many suitcases are you bringing?

CAREFUL — The word *what* is not always an interrogative adjective. It can also be an interrogative pronoun (see *What is an Interrogative Pronoun?*, p. 153). When it is a pronoun, *what* (**qué**) is not followed by a noun.

  What is on the table?

  |
  interrogative pronoun
  ¿Qué hay en la mesa?

The expression "how many" is not always an interrogative adjective. It can also be an interrogative pronoun. When it is a pronoun, *how many* (**cuánto**) is not followed by a noun.

  How many do you need?
  |_____|_____|
  interrogative pronoun
  ¿Cuántos necesitas?

It is important that you distinguish interrogative adjectives from interrogative pronouns because, in Spanish, sometimes different words are used and they follow different rules.

— *REVIEW* —

A. Circle the interrogative adjectives in the sentences below.
- Draw an arrow from the interrogative adjective to the noun it modifies.

1. Which book is yours?
2. Please tell me what exercises are due tomorrow.
3. Which house do you live in?

B. Circle the interrogative adjectives in the sentences below.
- Draw an arrow from the interrogative adjective to the noun it modifies.
- Indicate if the noun modified is singular (S) or plural (P).
- Fill in the Spanish interrogative adjective in the Spanish sentences below.

1. How many shirts did you buy?

   NOUN MODIFIED IN SPANISH: feminine   S   P

   ¿ _____ camisas compraste?

2. How much wine are you bringing to the party?

   NOUN MODIFIED IN SPANISH: masculine   S   P

   ¿ _____ vino traes a la fiesta?

3. How many telephones are there in your house?

   NOUN MODIFIED IN SPANISH: masculine   S   P

   ¿ _____ teléfonos hay en tu casa?

4. How much salad do you want?

   NOUN MODIFIED IN SPANISH: feminine   S   P

   ¿ _____ ensalada quieres?

CHAPTER

32

WHAT IS A DEMONSTRATIVE ADJECTIVE?

A **DEMONSTRATIVE ADJECTIVE** is a word used
to point out a noun.

This book is interesting.
|
points out the noun *book*

IN ENGLISH

The demonstrative adjectives are ***this*** and ***that*** in the singular and ***these*** and ***those*** in the plural. They are rare
examples of English adjectives agreeing in number with
the noun they modify: *this* changes to *these* and *that*
changes to *those* when they modify a plural noun.

SINGULAR	PLURAL
this cat	*these* cats
that man	*those* men

This and *these* refer to persons or objects near the speaker, and *that* and *those* refer to persons or objects away
from the speaker.

IN SPANISH

There are three sets of demonstrative adjectives that
change to agree in gender and number with the nouns
they modify.

In order to say *"this* house" or *"that* room" you start by
determining where the person or object is in relation to the
speaker or the person spoken to. Then, determine the gender and number of the noun you wish to point out and
make the demonstrative adjective agree with that noun.

1. noun near the speaker (*this, these*) → a form of **este**

   ▪ noun modified is masculine singular → **este**

   > **Este** cuarto es grande.
   >> **Cuarto** *(room)* is masculine singular, so the word for
   >> "this" must be masculine singular.
   >
   > *This room is large.*

   ▪ noun modified is feminine singular → **esta**

   > **Esta** casa es grande.
   >> **Casa** *(house)* is feminine singular, so the word for
   >> "this" must be feminine singular.
   >
   > *This house is large.*

- noun modified is masculine plural → **estos**

    Estos cuartos son grandes.
    > **Cuartos** *(rooms)* is masculine plural, so the word for
    > "these" must be masculine plural.

    These rooms are large.

- noun modified is feminine plural → **estas**

    Estas casas son grandes.
    > **Casas** *(houses)* is feminine plural, so the word for
    > "these" must be feminine plural.

    These houses are large.

2. noun near the person spoken to *(that, those)* → a form of **ese**

- noun modified is masculine singular → **ese**

    Ese cuarto es grande.
    > **Cuarto** *(room)* is masculine singular, so the word for
    > "that" must be masculine singular.

    That room is large.

- noun modified is feminine singular → **esa**

    Esa casa es grande.
    > **Casa** *(house)* is feminine singular, so the word for
    > "that" must be feminine singular.

    That house is large.

- noun modified is masculine plural → **esos**

    Esos cuartos son grandes.
    > **Cuartos** *(rooms)* is masculine plural, so the word for
    > "those" must be masculine plural.

    Those rooms are large.

- noun modified is feminine plural → **esas**

    Esas casas son grandes.
    > **Casas** *(houses)* is feminine plural, so the word for
    > "those" must be feminine plural.

    Those houses are large.

3. noun away from both the speaker and the person spoken to *(that, those)* → a form of **aquel**

    Since English does not have this third set of demonstrative adjectives, there is no good translation for them. Sometimes "over there" is added to imply the distance.

- noun modified is masculine singular → **aquel**

    Aquel cuarto es grande.
    > **Cuarto** *(room)* is masculine singular, so the word for
    > "that" must be masculine singular.

    That room (over there) is large.

- noun modified is feminine singular → **aquella**

    Aquella casa es grande.

    > Casa *(house)* is feminine singular, so the word for "that" must be feminine singular.

    That house (over there) is large.

- noun modified is masculine plural → **aquellos**

    Aquellos cuartos son grandes.

    > Cuartos *(rooms)* is masculine plural, so the word for "those" must be masculine plural.

    Those rooms (over there) are large.

- noun modified is feminine plural → **aquellas**

    Aquellas casas son grandes.

    > Casas *(houses)* is feminine plural, so the word for "those" must be feminine plural.

    Those houses (over there) are large.

CAREFUL — These three sets of demonstrative adjectives may also function as demonstrative pronouns (see *What is a Demonstrative Pronoun?*, p. 161). As demonstrative pronouns they are not followed by a noun.

— REVIEW —

Circle the demonstrative adjectives in the sentences below.
- Draw an arrow from the demonstrative adjective to the noun it modifies.
- Circle if the noun modified is singular (S) or plural (P).
- Fill in the Spanish demonstrative adjective in the Spanish sentences below.

1. They prefer that restaurant.

    NOUN MODIFIED IN SPANISH: masculine   S   P

    Prefieren _____ restaurante.

2. Those houses over there are very expensive.

    NOUN MODIFIED IN SPANISH: feminine   S   P

    _____ casas son muy caras.

3. I bought these shoes in Spain.

    NOUN MODIFIED IN SPANISH: masculine   S   P

    Compré _____ zapatos en España.

4. Do you want this magazine?

    NOUN MODIFIED IN SPANISH: feminine   S   P

    ¿Quieres _____ revista?

CHAPTER

33

WHAT IS MEANT BY COMPARISON OF ADJECTIVES?

The term COMPARISON OF ADJECTIVES is used when two or more persons or things have the same quality (height, size, color, any characteristic) indicated by a descriptive adjective and we want to show which of these persons or things has a greater, lesser, or equal degree of that quality.

comparison of adjectives

Paul is *tall* but Mary is *taller*.

adjective   adjective
modifies *Paul*   modifies *Mary*

Both nouns, Paul and Mary, have the same quality indicated by the adjective *tall*, and we want to show that Mary has a greater degree of that quality (i.e., she is *taller* than Paul).

In English and in Spanish there are two types of comparison: comparative and superlative.

───────────── **COMPARATIVE** ─────────────

The comparative compares a quality of a person or thing with the same quality in another person or thing. The comparison can indicate that one or the other has more, less, or the same amount of that quality.

IN ENGLISH

Let's go over the three degrees of comparison:

1. The comparison of GREATER DEGREE (more) is formed differently depending on the length of the adjective being compared.

   ■ short adjective + *-er* + *than*

      Paul is tall*er than* Mary.
      Susan is old*er than* her sister.

   ■ *more* + longer adjective + *than*

      Mary is *more* intelligent *than* John.
      His car is *more* expensive *than* ours.

2. The comparison of LESSER DEGREE (less) is formed as follows: *not as* + adjective *as*, or *less* + adjective + *than*.

Mary is *not as* tall *as* Paul.
My car is *less* expensive *than* your car.

3. The comparison of EQUAL DEGREE (same) is formed as follows: *as* + adjective + *as*.

Robert is *as* tall *as* Mary.
My car is *as* expensive *as* his car.

IN SPANISH

There are the same three degrees of comparison of adjectives as in English.

Like all Spanish adjectives, Spanish comparative adjectives agree with the noun they modify. In the case of comparative adjectives that describe more than one noun, they agree in gender and number with the subject.

1. The comparison of GREATER DEGREE is formed as follows: **más** *(more)* + adjective + **que** *(than)*.

María es **más alta que** Juan.
    |
agrees with subject → María
*Mary is **taller than** John.*

2. The comparison of LESSER DEGREE is formed as follows: **menos** *(less)* + adjective + **que** *(than)*.

Juan es **menos alto que** María.
    |
agrees with subject → Juan
*John is **less tall than** Mary.*

3. The comparison of EQUAL DEGREE is formed as follows: **tan** *(as)* + adjective + **como** *(as)*.

María es **tan alta como** Roberto.
    |
agrees with subject → María
*María is **as tall as** Robert.*

———— SUPERLATIVE ————

The superlative is used to stress the highest or lowest degrees of a quality.

IN ENGLISH

Let's go over the two degrees of the superlative:

1. The superlative of GREATEST DEGREE is formed differently depending on the length of the adjective.

   ▪ *the* + short adjective + *-est*

Mary is *the* smart*est*.
My car is *the* cheap*est* on the market.

■ *the most* + long adjective 80

Mary is *the most* intelligent.
His car is *the most* expensive.

2. The superlative of LOWEST DEGREE is formed as follows:
the least + adjective.

Paul is *the least* active.
Her car is *the least* expensive of all.

IN SPANISH

There are the same two degrees of the superlative: 90

1. The superlative of GREATEST DEGREE is formed as follows:
el, la, los or **las** (depending on the gender and number
of the noun described) + **más** *(most)* + adjective.

Juan es **el más bajo** de la familia.
       masc. sing.
*John is **the shortest** in the family.*

María es **la más alta**.
    fem. sing.
*Mary is **the tallest**.* 100

Carlos y Roberto son **los más divertidos** de la clase.
      masc. pl.
*Charles and Robert are **the funniest** in the class.*

Teresa y Gloria son **las más inteligentes**.
     fem. pl.
*Teresa and Gloria are **the most intelligent**.*

2. The superlative of LOWEST DEGREE is formed as follows:
el, la, los or **las** (depending on the gender and number
of the noun described) + **menos** *(least)* + adjective. 110

Mi coche es **el menos caro**.
     masc. sing.
*My car is **the least expensive**.*

CAREFUL — In English and in Spanish, a few adjectives have
irregular forms of comparison which you will have to memorize individually.

ADJECTIVE	Esta manzana es **buena**.
	*This apple is **good**.*
COMPARATIVE	Esta manzana es **mejor**.
	*This apple is **better**.*
SUPERLATIVE	Esta manzana es **la mejor**.
	*This apple is **the best**.*

— *R E V I E W* —

Underline the comparative and superlative adjectives in the sentences below.
- Draw an arrow from the adjective to the noun it modifies.
- Circle the various degrees of comparison: superlative (S), comparative of greater degree (C+), comparative of equal degree (C=), or comparative of lesser degree (C-).

1. The teacher is older than the students.　S　C+　C=　C-

2. He is less intelligent than I am.　　　　S　C+　C=　C-

3. Mary is as tall as Paul.　　　　　　　　S　C+　C=　C-

4. That boy is the worst in the school.　　S　C+　C=　C-

5. Paul is a better student than Mary.　　S　C+　C=　C-

WHAT IS AN ADVERB?

An ADVERB is a word that describes a verb, an adjective, or another adverb. It indicates manner, degree, time, place.[1]

> Mary drives *well*.
> | |
>   verb adverb
>
> The house is *very* big.
> | |
>   adverb adjective
>
> The girl ran *too quickly*.
> | |
>   adverb adverb

IN ENGLISH

There are different types of adverbs:

- an ADVERB OF MANNER answers the question *how?* Adverbs of manner are the most common and they are easy to recognize because they end with *-ly*.

  Mary sings *beautifully*.

  Beautifully describes the verb *sings*; it tells you how Mary sings.

- an ADVERB OF DEGREE answers the question *how much?*

  Paul did *well* on the exam.

- an ADVERB OF TIME answers the question *when?*

  He will come *soon*.

- an ADVERB OF PLACE answers the question *where?*

  The children were left *behind*.

IN SPANISH

Most adverbs of manner can be recognized by the ending -mente which corresponds to the English ending *-ly*.

fácilmente	*easily*
naturalmente	*naturally*
rápidamente	*rapidly*

---

[1]In English and in Spanish, the structure for comparing adverbs is the same as the structure for comparing adjectives (see *What is Meant by Comparison of Adjectives?*, p. 113).

You will have to memorize adverbs as vocabulary items. The most important fact for you to remember is that adverbs are INVARIABLE; ie., they never change form.

─────────── **ADVERB OR ADJECTIVE?** ───────────

Because adverbs are invariable and Spanish adjectives must agree with the noun they modify, it is important that you distinguish one from the other. When you write a sentence in Spanish, always make sure that adjectives agree with the nouns or pronouns they modify and that adverbs remain unchanged.

> *The **tall** girl talked **rapidly**.*
>
> *Tall* modifies the noun *girl;* it is an adjective. *Rapidly* modifies the verb *talked* (it describes how the girl talked); it is an adverb.
>
> La chica **alta** habló **rápidamente**.
>   fem. sing. adj.   adverb

> *The **tall** boy talked **rapidly**.*
>
> *Tall* modifies the noun *boy;* it is an adjective. *Rapidly* modifies the verb *talked* (it describes how the boy talked); it is an adverb.
>
> El chico **alto** habló **rápidamente**.
>   masc. sing. adj.   adverb

CAREFUL — Remember that in English *good* is an adjective since it modifies a noun and *well* is an adverb since it modifies a verb.

> The student writes *good* English.
> *Good* modifies the noun *English;* it is an adjective.

> The student writes *well*.
> *Well* modifies the verb *writes;* it is an adverb.

Likewise, in Spanish **bueno** is an adjective meaning *good;* **bien** is the adverb meaning *well*.

> *The **good** students speak Spanish **well**.*
>   adjective   adverb
>
> Los estudiantes **buenos** hablan español **bien**.
>   masc. pl. adj.   adverb

— *REVIEW* —

Circle the adverbs in the sentences below.
- Draw an arrow from the adverb to the word it modifies.

1. The students arrived early.

2. Paul learned the lesson really quickly.

3. The students were too tired to study.

4. He has a reasonably secure income.

5. Mary is a good student who speaks Spanish very well.

WHAT IS A CONJUNCTION?

A **CONJUNCTION** is a word that links two
or more words or groups of words.

He had to choose between good *and* evil.
|
conjunction

They left *because* they were bored.
|
conjunction

IN ENGLISH

There are two kinds of conjunctions: coordinating and
subordinating.

- a **COORDINATING CONJUNCTION** joins words, phrases (groups
of words without a verb), and clauses (groups of words
with a verb) that are equal; it *coordinates* elements of
equal rank. The major coordinating conjunctions are
and, but, or, nor, for, and *yet.*

good *or* evil
| |
word word

over the river *and* through the woods
|_____| |_____|
phrase   phrase

They invited us *but* we couldn't go.
|_____| |_____|
clause   clause

In the last example, each of the two clauses, "they
invited us" and "we couldn't go," expresses a complete
thought; each clause is, therefore, a complete sentence
which could stand alone. When a clause expresses a
complete sentence it is called a **MAIN CLAUSE**. In the
above sentence, the coordinating conjunction *but* links
two main clauses.

- a **SUBORDINATING CONJUNCTION** joins a main clause to
a dependent clause; it *subordinates* one clause to another. A **DEPENDENT CLAUSE** does not express a complete
thought; it is, therefore, not a complete sentence and
cannot stand alone. There are various types of dependent clauses. A clause introduced by a subordinating

conjunction is called a SUBORDINATE CLAUSE. Typical subordinating conjunctions are *before, after, since, although,
because, if, unless, so that, while, that,* and *when.*

subordinate clause   main clause   40

Although we were invited, we didn't go.
|
subordinating
conjunction

main clause   subordinate clause

They left *because* they were bored.
|
subordinating
conjunction

main clause subordinate clause   50

He said *that* he was tired.
|
subordinating
conjunction

In the above examples, "although we were invited,"
"because they were bored," and "that he was tired," are all
subordinate clauses. They are not complete sentences and
each is introduced by a subordinating conjunction.

Notice that the subordinate clause may come either at
the beginning of the sentence or after the main clause.   60

IN SPANISH ──────────────────────────

Conjunctions must be memorized as vocabulary items. Just
as adverbs and prepositions, conjunctions are INVARIABLE;
i.e., they never change their form.

— REVIEW —

Circle the coordinating and subordinating conjunctions in the
sentences below.
- Underline the words each conjunction serves to coordinate or
  to subordinate.

1. Mary and Paul were going to study French or Spanish.

2. She did not study because she was too tired.

3. Not only had he forgotten his ticket, but he had forgotten
   his passport as well.

WHAT IS A PREPOSITION?

A **PREPOSITION** is a word that shows the relationship of one word (usually a noun or pronoun) to another word (usually another noun or pronoun) in the sentence.

prepositional phrase

Paul has an appointment *after* school.

preposition   object of preposition

The noun or pronoun following the preposition is called the **OBJECT OF THE PREPOSITION**. The preposition plus its object is called a **PREPOSITIONAL PHRASE**.

IN ENGLISH ──────────────────────────────

Prepositions normally indicate location, direction, or time.

- prepositions showing location or direction

    Paul was *in* the car.
    Mary put the books *on* the table.
    The students came directly *from* class.
    Mary went *to* school.

- prepositions showing time and date

    Many Spanish people go on vacation *in* August.
    On Mondays, they go to the university.
    I'm meeting him *at* 4:30 today.
    We're studying *before* taking the exam.
    Most people work *from* nine *to* five.

Other frequently used prepositions are: *during, since, with, between, of, about*. Some prepositions are made up of more than a single word: *because of, in front of, instead of, due to, in spite of, on account of*.

IN SPANISH ──────────────────────────────

You will have to memorize prepositions as vocabulary, paying special attention to their meaning and use. Prepositions are **INVARIABLE**, that is, they never change form.

CAREFUL — Prepositions are tricky. Every language uses prepositions differently. Do not assume that the same preposition is used in Spanish as in English, or even that a preposition will be needed in Spanish when you must use one in English and vice versa.

ENGLISH	SPANISH
CHANGE OF PREPOSITION	
to laugh *at*	reirse **de** *(of)*
to consist *of*	consistir **en** *(in)*
PREPOSITION	**NO PREPOSITION**
to look *for*	buscar
to look *at*	mirar
NO PREPOSITION	**PREPOSITION**
to leave	salir **de**
to enter	entrar **en**

40

50

A dictionary will usually give you the verb and the preposition which follows it, when one is required.

Do not translate an English verb + preposition with a word-for-word Spanish equivalent (see pp. 21-2).

— REVIEW —

Circle the prepositions in the following sentences.

1. I will call you toward the end of the week.

2. His family had come from Peru last year.

3. The teacher walked around the room as she talked.

4. These days many men and women work at home.

5. The garden between the two houses was very small.

CHAPTER

37

WHAT ARE OBJECTS?

1   OBJECTS are nouns or pronouns indicating towards what
     or whom the action of the verb is directed.

Paul writes a *letter.*
| |
verb   object

He speaks to *Mary.*
| |
verb   object

The boy left with *his father.*
| |
verb   object

10   We will study the three types of objects separately: direct
     object, indirect object, and object of a preposition. Since noun
     and pronoun objects are identified by using the same set of
     questions, we have limited the examples in this section to
     noun objects. For examples with pronoun objects see *What are
     Direct and Indirect Object Pronouns?*, p. 131 and *What are Object of
     Preposition Pronouns?*, p. 139.

─────────────────── **DIRECT OBJECT** ───────────────────

IN ENGLISH

20   A direct object is a noun or pronoun that receives the
     action of the verb directly, without a preposition between
     the verb and the noun or pronoun. It answers the ques-
     tion *whom?* or *what?* asked after the verb.[1]

John sees *Mary.*
John sees *whom?* Mary.
Mary is the direct object.

John writes *a letter.*
John writes *what?* A letter.
30   *A letter* is the direct object.

Verbs can be classified as to whether or not they take a
direct object.

■ a TRANSITIVE VERB is a verb that takes a direct object. It is
  indicated by the abbreviation *v.t. (verbo transitivo)* in
  Spanish dictionaries.

---

[1]In this section, we will consider active sentences only (see *What is Meant by Active and Passive Voice?*, p. 91).

The boy *threw* the ball.

transitive   direct object

- an **INTRANSITIVE VERB** is a verb that does not require a direct object. It is indicated by the abbreviation *v.i.* *(verbo intransitivo)* in Spanish dictionaries.

Paul *is sleeping.*

intransitive

IN SPANISH

As in English, a direct object is a noun or pronoun that receives the action of the verb directly. It answers the question ¿**quién**? *(whom?)* or ¿**qué**? *(what?)* asked after the verb.

Juan escribe **una carta.**
John writes *what?* A letter (**una carta**).
Una carta is the direct object.
John writes a letter.

In Spanish a direct object noun referring to a person is preceded by the word "a". This is called the **PERSONAL a**. It does not have an English translation.

Juan ve **a María.**

personal **a** + direct object noun (person)
John sees Mary.

Juan ve **a las muchachas.**

personal **a** + direct object noun (persons)
John sees the girls.

Juan ve **al hombre.**

personal **a** + **el** + direct object noun (person)
John sees the man.

Juan ve **la casa.**

no personal **a** required, direct object noun (thing)
John sees the house.

───────────── **INDIRECT OBJECT** ─────────────

IN ENGLISH

An indirect object is a noun or pronoun that receives the action of the verb indirectly. It answers the question *to whom?* or *to what?* asked after the verb.

John wrote *his brother.*
He wrote *to whom?* His brother.
His brother is the indirect object.

Sometimes the word *to* is included in the English sentence.[1]

John spoke *to Paul and Mary.*
John speaks *to whom?* To Paul and Mary.
Paul and Mary are two indirect objects.

IN SPANISH

As in English, an indirect object is a noun or pronoun that receives the action of the verb indirectly with the preposition a *(to)* relating it to the verb. It answers the question ¿a quién? *(to whom)* or ¿a qué? *(to what?)* asked after the verb.

In Spanish an indirect object pronoun is added in a sentence with an indirect object noun which refers to a person. For instance, **le** is used when the indirect object noun is singular and **les** is used when the indirect object noun is plural (see *What are Direct and Indirect Object Pronouns?*, p. 131).

Juan **le** escribió a su hermano.
singular
(word-for-word: *John (to him) wrote to his brother*)
John wrote (to) his brother.

Juan **les** habló a Pablo y a María.
plural
(word-for-word: *John (to them) spoke to Paul and Mary*)
John spoke (to) Paul and Mary.

— **SENTENCES WITH A DIRECT AND AN INDIRECT OBJECT** —

A sentence may contain both a direct object and an indirect object which may be either nouns or pronouns. In this section we shall speak only of nouns as objects.

IN ENGLISH

When a sentence has both a direct and an indirect object, the following two word orders are possible:

1. subject (S) + verb (V) + indirect object (IO) + direct object (DO)

[1]In English "to Paul and Mary" is called a PREPOSITIONAL PHRASE because it is a phrase that begins with the preposition *to*; in this book we refer to noun and pronoun objects of the preposition *to* as indirect objects since that is how they function in Spanish.

John gave his sister a gift.

   S   V   IO   DO

> *Who* gave a gift? John.
> *John* is the subject.
>
> John gave *what?* A gift.
> *A gift* is the direct object.
>
> John gave a gift *to whom?* His sister.
> *His sister* is the indirect object.

2. subject + verb + direct object + *to* + indirect object

John gave a gift to his sister.

   S   V   DO   IO

The first structure, under 1, is the most common. However, because there is no "*to*" preceding the indirect object, it is more difficult to identify its function than in the second structure.

Regardless of the word order, the function of the words in these two sentences is the same because they answer the same question. Be sure to ask the questions to establish the function of words in a sentence.

IN SPANISH

Unlike English, when a sentence has both a direct and an indirect object noun there is only one word order possible (structure 2): subject + **le** or **les** + verb + direct object + **a** *(to)* + indirect object.

Juan **le** dio **un regalo a su hermana.**

   S **le** V   DO **a**   IO

(word-for-word: *John (to her) gave a gift to his sister*)
John gave his sister a gift.
John gave a gift to his sister.

--------- **OBJECT OF A PREPOSITION** ---------

IN ENGLISH

An object of a preposition is a noun or pronoun that follows a preposition and is related to it. It answers the question *whom?* or *what?* asked after the preposition.

> John is leaving *with Mary.*
> John is leaving *with whom?* With Mary.
> *Mary* is the object of the preposition *with.*
>
> The baby eats *with a spoon.*
> The baby eats *with what?* With a spoon.
> *A spoon* is the object of the preposition *with.*

130

140

150

160

IN SPANISH

As in English, an object of a preposition is a noun or pronoun that follows a preposition and is related to it. It answers the question ¿quién? or ¿qué? asked after the preposition.

> Pablo sale con María.
> *Paul is leaving with Mary.*

> Juan trabaja para el Sr. Jones.
> *John works for Mr. Jones.*

———— RELATIONSHIP OF A VERB TO ITS OBJECT ————

The relationship between a verb and its object is often different in English and Spanish. For example, a verb may take an object of a preposition in English but a direct object in Spanish. Therefore, when you learn a Spanish verb, it is important to find out if it is followed by a preposition, and if so, which one. Your textbook, as well as dictionaries, will indicate when a Spanish verb needs a preposition before an object.

Here are differences you are likely to encounter.

1. ENGLISH: object of a preposition → SPANISH: direct object

> *I am looking for the book.*
> FUNCTION IN ENGLISH: object of a preposition
> I am looking *for what?* The book.
> *The book* is the object of the preposition *for.*

> Busco el libro.
> FUNCTION IN SPANISH: direct object
> ¿Qué busco? El libro.
> Since buscar *(to look for)* is not followed by a preposition, it takes a direct object.

Many common verbs require an object of a preposition in English, but a direct object in Spanish.

to look for	buscar
to look at	mirar
to ask for	pedir
to listen to	escuchar
to wait for	esperar
to wait on	servir

2. ENGLISH: direct object → SPANISH: object of a preposition

> *John remembers his apartment in Madrid.*
> Function in English: direct object
> John remember *what?* His apartment.
> *His apartment* is the direct object.

Juan se acuerda **de su apartamento** en Madrid.
Function in Spanish: object of a preposition
¿**De qué** se acuerda Juan? **De su apartamento.**
(word-for-word: *Of what does John remember?*
Of his apartment.) The verb **acordarse** *(to remember)* is followed by the preposition **de** *(of)*; it requires an object of
the preposition **de.**

210

A few common verbs require a direct object in English
but an object of a preposition in Spanish.

to enjoy	gozar **de**
to enter	entrar **en**
to forget	olvidarse **de**
to leave	salir **de**
to marry	casarse **con**
to play	jugar **a**
to remember	acordarse **de**

220

CAREFUL — Always identify the function of a word within
the language in which you are working; do not mix English
and Spanish patterns.

─────────────────── **SUMMARY** ───────────────────

Your ability to recognize the three types of objects is essential. A different Spanish pronoun is used for the English pronoun *him* depending on whether *him* is a direct object (**lo**),
an indirect object (**le**), or an object of a preposition (**él**).

230

The different types of objects in a sentence can be identified by establishing whether they answer a question which
requires a preposition or not and, if so, which one.

DIRECT OBJECT — An object that receives the action of the
verb directly.

INDIRECT OBJECT — An object that receives the action of the
verb indirectly, sometimes with the preposition *to.*

240

OBJECT OF A PREPOSITION — An object that receives the action
of the verb through a preposition.

— *REVIEW* —

Find the objects in the sentences below:
- Next to Q, write the question you need to ask to find the object.
- Next to A, write the answer to the question you just asked.
- Circle the kind of object it is: direct object (DO), indirect object (IO) or object of a preposition (OP).

1. The children took a shower.

   Q: _____

   A: _____ DO   IO   OP

2. They ate the meal with their friends.

   Q: _____

   A: _____ DO   IO   OP

   Q: _____

   A: _____ DO   IO   OP

3. He sent a present to his brother.

   Q: _____

   A: _____ DO   IO   OP

   Q: _____

   A: _____ DO   IO   OP

WHAT ARE DIRECT AND INDIRECT OBJECT PRONOUNS?

Pronouns used as direct and indirect objects
are called OBJECT PRONOUNS.

> Paul saw *her*.
>> Paul saw whom? ANSWER: Her.
>> *Her* is the object of the verb *saw*.

Pronouns change according to their function in the sentence. Pronouns used as subjects are studied in *What is a Subject Pronoun?*, p. 27. We use subject pronouns when we conjugate verbs (see *What is a Verb Conjugation?*, p. 35). Object pronouns are used when a pronoun is either a direct object, indirect object, or object of a preposition (see *What are Objects?*, p. 124; *What are Object of Preposition Pronouns?*, p. 139).

IN ENGLISH

Most object pronouns are different from subject pronouns, but the same pronouns are used as direct objects and indirect objects.

	SUBJECT	OBJECT
SINGULAR		
1ˢᵗ PERSON	I	me
2ⁿᵈ PERSON	you	you
3ʳᵈ PERSON	he	him
	she	her
	it	it
PLURAL		
1ˢᵗ PERSON	we	us
2ⁿᵈ PERSON	you	you
3ʳᵈ PERSON	they	them

Let us look at a few examples.

> She saw *me*.
>> direct object → object pronoun

> He lent *me* the car.
>> indirect object → object pronoun

In English, the object pronoun is placed after the verb.

IN SPANISH ————————————————————————————

As in English, the pronouns used as objects are different from the ones used as subjects. Unlike English, however, the form of an object pronoun often changes depending on whether it is a direct or an indirect object.

In Spanish, the direct and indirect object pronouns are usually placed before the verb. Consult your textbook.

——————— **SPANISH DIRECT OBJECT PRONOUNS** ———————

First, you have to establish that the Spanish verb takes a direct object. Remember that English and Spanish verbs don't always take the same type of objects and that when working in Spanish you have to establish the type of object required by the Spanish verb (see p. 128).

To simplify our examples in this section we have chosen the verb *to see* (**ver**) because both the English and the Spanish verbs take a direct object.

Let us look at the Spanish direct object pronouns to see how they are selected. Since the pattern for the direct object pronouns *me, you* (**tú** and **vosotros** forms), *him, her* and *us* is different from the pattern of *it, them,* and *you* (**usted** and **ustedes** forms), we have divided the Spanish direct object pronouns into these two categories.

———— **ME, YOU (TÚ AND VOSOTROS FORMS), HIM, HER, US** ————

The direct object pronouns equivalent to *me, you, him, her,* and *us* are a question of learning vocabulary. Just select the form you need from the chart below.

DIRECT OBJECTS	
me	me
you [tú form]	te
you [vosotros form]	os
him	lo
her	la
us	nos

Here are some examples.

*John sees **me**.*
  1. IDENTIFY THE VERB: *to see* (**ver**)
  2. IDENTIFY PRONOUN OBJECT: *me*
  3. FUNCTION OF PRONOUN IN SPANISH: direct object
  4. SELECTION: **me**
Juan **me** ve.

John sees you.
John **te** ve. [tú form]
John **os** ve. [**vosotros** form]

*Do you see John? Yes, I see **him**.*
¿Ves a Juan? Sí, **lo** veo.

*Do you see Mary? Yes, I see **her**.*
¿Ves a María? Sí, **la** veo.

*John sees **us**.*
John **nos** ve.

───────── IT, THEM, YOU (USTED AND USTEDES FORMS) ─────────

The direct object pronouns equivalent to *it*, *them* and *you*
change depending on the gender of the ANTECEDENT; that is,
the noun which they are replacing.

	DIRECT OBJECTS	
	MASCULINE	FEMININE
it	**lo**	**la**
you [usted form]	**lo**	**la**
them	**los**	**las**
you [ustedes form]	**los**	**las**

*Do you see the book? Yes, I see **it**.*
  1. ANTECEDENT: **el libro** *(book)*
  2. GENDER OF ANTECEDENT: masculine
  3. SELECTION: **lo**
¿Ves el libro? Sí, **lo** veo.

*Do you see the table? Yes, I see **it**.*
  1. ANTECEDENT: **la mesa** *(table)*
  2. GENDER OF ANTECEDENT: feminine
  3. SELECTION: **la**
¿Ves la mesa? Sí, **la** veo.

*Do you see the cars? Yes, I see **them**.*
  1. ANTECEDENT: **los coches** *(cars)*
  2. GENDER OF ANTECEDENT: masculine
  3. SELECTION: **los**
¿Ves los coches? Sí, **los** veo.

*Do you see the girls? Yes, I see **them**.*
  1. ANTECEDENT: **las chicas** *(girls)*
  2. GENDER OF ANTECEDENT: feminine
  3. SELECTION: **las**
¿Ves a las chicas? Sí, **las** veo.[1]

───────────────────

[1]The "a" before **chicas** is a personal a, not a preposition (see p. 125).

The pronoun *you* (formal) changes not only according to the gender of the person or persons you are addressing, but also according to whether you are addressing one or more persons.

> *Whom does John see? He sees you.* [when speaking to a male]
> 1. NUMBER & GENDER OF *YOU:* masculine singular
> 2. SELECTION: **lo**
>
> ¿A quién ve Juan? Juan **lo** ve.
>
> *Whom does John see? He sees you.* [when speaking to a female]
> 1. NUMBER & GENDER OF *YOU:* feminine singular
> 2. SELECTION: **la**
>
> ¿A quién ve Juan? Juan **la** ve.
>
> *Whom does John see? He sees you.* [when speaking to males or a mixed group]
> 1. NUMBER & GENDER OF *YOU:* masculine plural
> 2. SELECTION: **los**
>
> ¿A quién ve Juan? Juan **los** ve.
>
> *Whom does John see? He sees you.* [when speaking to females]
> 1. NUMBER & GENDER OF *YOU:* feminine plural
> 3. SELECTION: **las**
>
> ¿A quién ve Juan? Juan **las** ve.

──────────── **SPANISH INDIRECT OBJECT PRONOUNS** ────────────

First, you have to establish that the Spanish verb takes an indirect object. Remember that English and Spanish verbs don't always take the same type of objects and that when working in Spanish you have to establish the type of object required by the Spanish verb (see p. 128).

To simplify our examples in this section we have chosen the verb *to speak* (**hablar**) because both the English and the Spanish verbs take an indirect object.

Notice that unlike noun indirect objects which are always preceded by "a" in Spanish (see p. 126), pronoun indirect objects are not.

Let us look at the Spanish indirect object pronouns to see how they are selected. Since the pattern for the indirect object pronouns *me, you* (**tú** and **vosotros** forms), and *us* is different from the pattern of *him, her, you* (**usted** and **ustedes** forms), and *them*, we have divided the Spanish indirect object pronouns into these two categories.

──────────── **ME, YOU (TÚ AND VOSOTROS FORMS) US** ────────────

The indirect object pronouns equivalent to *me, you,* and *us* are the same as the direct object pronouns.

INDIRECT OBJECTS	
me	me
you [tú form]	te
us	nos
you [vosotros form]	os

John speaks to me.
1. IDENTIFY THE VERB: *to speak* (**hablar**)
2. IDENTIFY THE PRONOUN OBJECT: *me*
3. FUNCTION OF THE PRONOUN IN SPANISH: indirect object
4. SELECTION: **me**

Juan **me** habla.
   |
  indirect object pronoun

John speaks to you.
John **te** habla. [**tú** form]
John **os** habla. [**vosotros** persons]

John speaks to us.
John **nos** habla.

─────── **HIM, HER, YOU (USTED AND USTEDES FORMS), THEM** ───────

The indirect object pronouns equivalent to *him, her, you,* and *them* are a question of learning vocabulary. Just select the form you need from the chart below.

INDIRECT OBJECTS	
him, her, you [usted form]	le
them, you [ustedes form]	les

To whom is John speaking? John is speaking to him.
1. IDENTIFY THE VERB: *to speak* (**hablar**)
2. IDENTIFY THE PRONOUN OBJECT: *him*
3. FUNCTION OF THE PRONOUN IN SPANISH: indirect object
4. SELECTION: **le**

¿A quién **le** habla Juan? Juan **le** habla.[1]

Are you speaking to Mary? Yes, I am speaking to her.
¿**Le** hablas a María? Sí, **le** hablo.

To whom is John speaking? He is speaking to you. [one person]
1. IDENTIFY THE VERB: *to speak* (**hablar**)
2. IDENTIFY THE PRONOUN OBJECT: *you*
3. FUNCTION OF PRONOUN IN SPANISH: indirect object
4. SELECTION: **le**

¿A quién **le** habla Juan? Le habla.

170

180

190

200

─────────────

[1]For the inclusion of "**le**" in the question, see p. 126.

To whom is John speaking? John is speaking to them.
1. IDENTIFY THE VERB: *to speak* (**hablar**)
2. IDENTIFY THE PRONOUN OBJECT: *them*
3. FUNCTION OF PRONOUN IN SPANISH: indirect object
4. SELECTION: **les**

¿A quiénes **les** habla Juan? Juan **les** habla.

To whom is John speaking? He's speaking to you. [many persons]
1. IDENTIFY THE VERB: *to speak* (**hablar**)
2. IDENTIFY THE PRONOUN OBJECT: *you*
3. FUNCTION OF PRONOUN IN SPANISH: indirect object
4. SELECTION: **les**

¿A quiénes **les** habla Juan? **Les** habla.

In order to distinguish **le** meaning *to him* from **le** meaning *to her* or *to you,* the phrase **a él, a ella,** or **a usted** can be added to the end of the sentence.

Juan **le** habla **a él.**	*John speaks to him.*
Juan **le** habla **a ella.**	*John speaks to her.*
Juan **le** habla **a usted.**	*John speaks to you.*

In order to distinguish **les** meaning *to them* (masculine or feminine) and *to you,* the phrase **a ellos, a ellas,** or **a ustedes** can be added to the end of the sentence.

Juan **les** habla **a ellos.**	*John speaks to them.*
	[group of males or a mixed group]
Juan **les** habla **a ellas.**	*John speaks to them.*
	[group of females]
Juan **les** habla **a ustedes.**	*John speaks to you.*

───────────── **SUMMARY** ─────────────

As you can see from the various charts in this chapter:

1. The following pronouns have the same form when used as direct and indirect objects.

DIRECT AND INDIRECT OBJECTS	
me	me
you [tú form]	te
we	nos
you [vosotros form]	os

2. The following pronouns have different forms when used as direct and indirect objects. 240

	DIRECT OBJECTS	INDIRECT OBJECTS
him	lo	le
her	la	le
it	lo, la	le
you [usted form]	lo, la	le
them	los, las	les
you [ustedes form]	los, las	les

250

3. The following direct object pronouns have a different form depending on the gender of the antecedent.

	DIRECT OBJECTS	
	MASCULINE	FEMININE
it	lo	la
you [usted form]	lo	la
them	los	las
you [ustedes form]	los	las

260

Indirect objects do not distinguish between gender.

— *REVIEW* —

Underline the object pronoun in the sentences below.

* Using the charts on pp. 136-7, circle the correct Spanish equivalent: direct object (DO), or indirect object (IO), masculine (M), feminine (F), singular (S), or plural (P).

1. Mary bought the book and then she read it.

FUNCTION OF PRONOUN IN ENGLISH: DO   IO

FUNCTION OF PRONOUN IN SPANISH: DO   IO

ANTECEDENT IN ENGLISH: _____

NUMBER OF ANTECEDENT IN SPANISH: S   P

GENDER OF ANTECEDENT IN SPANISH: masculine

María compró el libro y después _____ leyó.

2. Juan bought some magazines and then he read them.

FUNCTION OF PRONOUN IN ENGLISH: DO   IO

FUNCTION OF PRONOUN IN SPANISH: DO   IO

ANTECEDENT IN ENGLISH: _____

NUMBER OF ANTECEDENT IN SPANISH: S   P

GENDER OF ANTECEDENT IN SPANISH: feminine

Juan compró algunas revistas y después _____ leyó.

3. The teacher spoke to them about the exam yesterday.

FUNCTION OF PRONOUN IN ENGLISH: DO   IO

FUNCTION OF PRONOUN IN SPANISH: DO   IO

NUMBER OF ANTECEDENT IN SPANISH: S   P

La profesora _____ habló del examen ayer.

4. Did you write Paul? No, but I will write him today.

FUNCTION OF PRONOUN IN ENGLISH: DO   IO

FUNCTION OF PRONOUN IN SPANISH: DO   IO

NUMBER OF PRONOUN: S   P

GENDER OF ANTECEDENT IN SPANISH: M   F

¿Le escribiste a Pablo? No, pero _____ escribiré hoy.

WHAT ARE OBJECT OF PREPOSITION PRONOUNS?

Object pronouns are also used as
OBJECTS OF A PREPOSITION.

They went out with *me*.
|
object of preposition *with*

IN ENGLISH ────────────────────────
The same forms of object pronouns are used for direct objects, indirect indirect objects and objects of a preposition (see *What are Direct and Indirect Object Pronouns?*, p. 131).

IN SPANISH ────────────────────────
Pronouns that are objects of a preposition (also called PREPOSITIONAL PRONOUNS) other than *to* have forms that are different from the forms used as direct and indirect objects. Unlike direct and indirect object pronouns which are placed before the verb, object of preposition pronouns are placed after the preposition.

Let us look at the Spanish object of preposition pronouns to see how they are selected. First, you have to establish that in Spanish there is a preposition, and if so, which one. Remember that English and Spanish verbs do not always use the same prepositions, if any, and that when working in Spanish you have to establish the preposition used in Spanish.

To simplify our examples in this section we have chosen English and Spanish verbs that take the same preposition.

Because the pattern of object of preposition pronouns for *me, you* (**tú**, **usted** and **ustedes** forms), *him,* and *her* are different from the pattern for *us, you* (**vosotros** form), and *them,* we have divided the Spanish object of preposition pronouns into these two categories.

──────── ME, YOU (TÚ, USTED AND USTEDES FORMS), HIM, HER ────────

The object of preposition pronouns equivalent to *me, you, him, her* are a question of learning vocabulary. Just select the form you need from the chart below.

OBJECTS OF A PREPOSITION	
me	mí
you [tú form]	ti
him	él
her	ella
you [usted form]	usted
you [ustedes form]	ustedes

Here are some examples.

Is the book for John? No, it's for me.
1. IDENTIFY THE PREPOSITION: *for*
2. IDENTIFY THE OBJECT OF THE PREPOSITION: *me*
3. SELECTION: **mí**

¿Es para Juan el libro? No, es para **mí.**

Is the book for John? Yes, it is for him.
1. IDENTIFY THE PREPOSITION: *for*
2. IDENTIFY THE OBJECT OF THE PREPOSITION: *him*
3. SELECTION: **él**

¿Es para Juan el libro? Sí, es **para él.**

Is the book for Mary? Yes, it is for her.
1. IDENTIFY THE PREPOSITION: *for*
2. IDENTIFY THE OBJECT OF THE PREPOSITION: *her*
3. SELECTION: **ella**

¿Es para María el libro? Sí, es **para ella.**

Is the book for John? No, it's for you. [one person]
1. IDENTIFY THE PREPOSITION: *for*
2. IDENTIFY THE OBJECT OF THE PREPOSITION: *you*
3. DISTINGUISH FORMAL FROM FAMILIAR: familiar
4. NUMBER OF THE PRONOUN *you*: singular
5. SELECTION: **ti**

¿Es para Juan el libro? No, es **para ti.**

Is the book for me? Yes, it is for you. [one person]
1. IDENTIFY THE PREPOSITION: *for*
2. IDENTIFY THE OBJECT OF THE PREPOSITION: *you*
3. DISTINGUISH FORMAL FROM FAMILIAR: formal
4. NUMBER OF THE PRONOUN *you*: singular
5. SELECTION: **usted**

¿Es para mí el libro? Sí, es **para usted.**

Are the books for us? Yes, they're for you. [more than one person]
1. IDENTIFY THE PREPOSITION: *for*
2. IDENTIFY THE OBJECT OF THE PREPOSITION: *you*
3. DISTINGUISH FORMAL FROM FAMILIAR: formal
4. NUMBER OF THE PRONOUN *you*: plural
5. SELECTION: **ustedes**

¿Son para nosotros los libros? Sí, son **para ustedes.**

—————————— Us, you (vosotros form), them ——————————

The object of preposition pronouns equivalent to *us, you,* and *them* change depending on the gender of the persons that they refer to.

80

	OBJECTS OF A PREPOSITION	
	MASCULINE	FEMININE
us	nosotros	nosotras
you	vosotros	vosotras
them	ellos	ellas

Are the books for John? No, they're for us. [group of males or mixed group]

   1. IDENTIFY THE PREPOSITION: *for*
   2. IDENTIFY THE OBJECT OF THE PREPOSITION: *us*
   3. GENDER OF THE PRONOUN *US*: masculine
   4. SELECTION: **nosotros**

90

¿Son para Juan los libros? No, son **para nosotros.**

Are the books for John? No, they're for us. [group of females]

   1. - 2. (see above)
   3. GENDER OF THE PRONOUN *US*: feminine
   4. SELECTION: **nosotras**

¿Son para Juan los libros? No, son **para nosotras.**

Are the books for John? No, they're for you. [group of males or mixed group]

   1. IDENTIFY THE PREPOSITION: *for*
   2. IDENTIFY THE OBJECT OF THE PREPOSITION: *you*
   3. DISTINGUISH FORMAL FROM FAMILIAR: familiar
   4. NUMBER OF THE PRONOUN *YOU*: plural
   5. GENDER OF THE PRONOUN *YOU*: masculine
   6. SELECTION: **vosotros**

100

¿Son para Juan los libros? No, son **para vosotros.**

Are the books for John? No, they're for you. [group of females]

   1. - 4. (see above)
   5. GENDER OF THE PRONOUN *YOU*: feminine
   6. SELECTION: **vosotras**

110

¿Son para Juan los libros? No, son **para vosotras.**

*Is the book for the children? Yes, it's **for them.***

   1. IDENTIFY THE PREPOSITION: *for*
   2. IDENTIFY THE OBJECT OF THE PREPOSITION: *them*
   3. GENDER OF THE PRONOUN *THEM*: masculine *(boys)*
   4. SELECTION: **ellos**

¿Es para los niños el libro? Sí, es **para ellos.**

*Is the book for Mary and Gloria? Yes, it's for **them.***
1. - 2. (see above)
3. GENDER OF THE PRONOUN *THEM*: feminine *(Mary and Gloria)*
4. SELECTION: **ellas**

¿Es para María y Gloria el libro? Sí, es **para ellas.**

CAREFUL — The English object of preposition pronouns for *it* or *them* referring to things has no Spanish equivalent.

— *REVIEW* —

Underline the object of preposition pronouns in the sentences below.
- Identify the number of the prepositional pronoun in Spanish: singular (S) or plural (P).
- Identify the gender of the prepositional pronoun in Spanish: masculine (M), feminine (F), gender unknown or doesn't matter (NA).
- Using the charts in this chapter, fill in the blank with the correct form of the prepositional pronoun.

1. Is this gift for Teresa and Ana? Yes, the gift is for them.
   NUMBER OF PREPOSITIONAL PRONOUN IN SPANISH: S   P
   GENDER OF PREPOSITIONAL PRONOUN IN SPANISH: M   F   NA

   ¿Es para Teresa y Ana el regalo? Sí, el regalo es para _____.

2. Is this gift from your mother? Yes, it's from her.
   NUMBER OF PREPOSITIONAL PRONOUN IN SPANISH: S   P
   GENDER OF PREPOSITIONAL PRONOUN IN SPANISH: M   F   NA

   ¿Es este regalo de su madre? Sí, es de _____.

3. Is this letter for John? No, it's for you [tú form].
   NUMBER OF PREPOSITIONAL PRONOUN IN SPANISH: S   P
   GENDER OF PREPOSITIONAL PRONOUN IN SPANISH: M   F   NA

   ¿Es esta carta para Juan? No, es para _____.

4. Is Mary going to the party with John? No, she's going with us.
   NUMBER OF PREPOSITIONAL PRONOUN IN SPANISH: S   P
   GENDER OF PREPOSITIONAL PRONOUN IN SPANISH: M   F   NA

   ¿Va María a la fiesta con Juan? No, va con _____.

WHAT ARE REFLEXIVE PRONOUNS AND VERBS?

A **REFLEXIVE VERB** is a verb which is accompanied
by a pronoun, called a **REFLEXIVE PRONOUN**, that serves
"to reflect" the action of the verb back to the subject.

subject   reflexive pronoun → the same person

She *cut herself* with the knife.

reflexive verb

IN ENGLISH

Many regular verbs can take on a reflexive meaning by
adding a reflexive pronoun.

The child *dresses* the doll.

regular verb

The child *dresses herself.*

verb + reflexive pronoun

Reflexive pronouns end with *-self* in the singular and
-selves in the plural.

	SUBJECT PRONOUN	REFLEXIVE PRONOUN
SINGULAR		
1ˢᵀ PERSON	I	myself
2ᴺᴰ PERSON	you	yourself
3ᴿᴰ PERSON	he	himself
	she	herself
	it	itself
PLURAL		
1ˢᵀ PERSON	we	ourselves
2ᴺᴰ PERSON	you	yourselves
3ᴿᴰ PERSON	they	themselves

As the subject changes so does the reflexive pronoun,
because they both refer to the same person or object.

I cut *myself.*
John and Mary blamed *themselves* for the accident.

Although the subject pronoun *you* is the same for the singular and plural, there is a difference in the reflexive pronouns: *yourself* (singular) is used when you are speaking to one person and *yourselves* (plural) is used when you are speaking to more than one.

> *Paul,* did *you* make *yourself* a sandwich?
> *Children,* make sure *you* wash *yourselves* properly.

Reflexive verbs can be in any tense: *I wash myself, I washed myself, I will wash myself,* etc.

IN SPANISH

As in English, Spanish reflexive verbs are formed with a verb and a reflexive pronoun.

Here are the Spanish reflexive pronouns:

SINGULAR

1ST PERSON	me	*myself*
2ND PERSON	te	*yourself* [tú form]
3RD PERSON	se	*himself, herself, yourself* [usted form]

PLURAL

1ST PERSON	nos	*ourselves*
2ND PERSON	os	*yourselves* [vosotros form]
3RD PERSON	se	*themselves, yourselves* [ustedes form]

In the dictionary, reflexive verbs are listed under the regular verb. For instance, under **lavar** *(to wash)* you will also find **lavarse** *(to wash oneself)*. Notice that the reflexive pronoun **se** is attached to the end of the infinitive to indicate a reflexive verb.

Look at the conjugation of **lavarse**. Notice two things:

1. as in English, the reflexive pronoun changes according to the person of the conjugation

2. unlike English, the reflexive pronoun is placed before the conjugated verb

	SUBJECT PRONOUN +	REFLEXIVE PRONOUN +	VERB
SINGULAR			
1ST PERSON	yo	me	lavo
2ND PERSON	tú	te	lavas
3RD PERSON	él / ella / usted	se	lava

PLURAL

1ˢᵀ PERSON	{ nosotros / nosotras }	nos lavamos
2ⁿᵈ PERSON	{ vosotros / vosotras }	os laváis
3ᴿᴰ PERSON	{ ellos / ellas / ustedes }	se lavan

Reflexive verbs can be conjugated in all tenses. The subject pronoun and reflexive pronoun remain the same regardless of the tense of the verb, only the verb form changes: él se lavará (future); él se lavó (preterite).

Reflexive verbs are common in Spanish. There are many English expressions that are not reflexive in English, but whose Spanish equivalent is a reflexive verb. You will have to memorize such expressions individually.

to wake up	despertarse *(to wake oneself up)*
to get up	levantarse *(to get oneself up)*
to go to bed	acostarse *(to put oneself to bed)*
to go to sleep	dormirse *(to put oneself to sleep)*
to get dressed	vestirse *(to dress oneself)*
to have a good time	divertirse *(to amuse oneself)*
to be worried	preocuparse *(to worry oneself)*

In all the examples above, the Spanish reflexive pronouns have a meaning equivalent to the English reflexive pronouns listed on p. 143 *(myself, yourself, himself,* etc.). This is not always the case. Spanish reflexive pronouns can also indicate reciprocal action.

—————————— **RECIPROCAL ACTION** ——————————

IN ENGLISH

To express reciprocal action, that is, an action between two or more persons or things, English uses a regular verb followed by the expression "each other."

The dog and the cat looked at *each other.*

The expression "each other" tells us that the action of "looking" was reciprocal, i.e. the dog looked at the cat and the cat looked at the dog.

Our children call *each other* every day.

The expression "each other" tells us that the action of "calling" is reciprocal, i.e. the various children call one another every day.

Reciprocal verbs are always plural since they require more than one person or thing be involved.

IN SPANISH

Spanish uses reflexive pronouns to express an action that is reciprocal.

> El perro y el gato se miraron.
> *The dog and the cat looked at **each other**.*

> Nuestros hijos se llaman cada día.
> *Our children call **each other** every day.*

Context will often indicate to you if the meaning of the Spanish pronoun is reflexive *(-self, -selves)* or reciprocal *(each other).*

> Las chicas se miran en el espejo.
>> The information "en el espejo" (in the mirror) leads us to believe that the girls are looking at themselves. Therefore, se is reflexive.
>
> *The girls look at **themselves** in the mirror.*
> |
> reflexive

However, when no information is given, the meaning of the Spanish sentence is ambiguous.

> Las chicas **se miran.**
> *The girls **look at themselves**.*   → REFLEXIVE
> *The girls **look at each other**.*   → RECIPROCAL

One way to avoid ambiguity, and to indicate that the meaning is reciprocal rather than reflexive, is to add an expression equivalent to "each other," such as "**el uno al otro**" (singular) or "**los unos a los otros**" (plural).

> El perro y el gato se miran **el uno al otro**.
> | | |
> masc. sing. masc. sing.   masc. sing.
> *The dog and the cat look at **each other**.*

> Los niños se miran **los unos a los otros**.
> | |
> masc. pl.   masc. pl.
> *The children look at **each other**.*

Consult your textbook for detailed explanations.

— *REVIEW* —

A. Fill in the appropriate English reflexive pronoun in the English sentences.
  - Fill in the appropriate Spanish reflexive pronoun in the Spanish sentences.

1. Mary cuts _____ a lot.

   María _____ corta muy a menudo.

2. Mary, you cut _____ a lot.

   María, tú _____ cortas muy a menudo.

3. We dress _____.

   Nosotros _____ vestimos.

4. The children wash_____every evening.

   Los niños _____ lavan todas las noches.

B. Fill in the appropriate English reflexive pronoun or the expression "each other."
  - Circle if the action is reflexive (Rx) or if the action is reciprocal (Rp).

1. The mother and son kissed _____.   Rx   Rp

2. Ambitious people push _____ to the limit.   Rx   Rp

3. To avoid being punished, the children blamed

   _____ for breaking the mirror.   Rx   Rp

4. When something goes wrong,
   I always blame _____.   Rx   Rp

5. Do you and your brother write

   _____ on e-mail?   Rx   Rp

CHAPTER

41

WHAT IS A POSSESSIVE PRONOUN?

A **POSSESSIVE PRONOUN** is a word that replaces a noun and indicates the possessor of that noun. The word *possessive* comes from *possess*, to own.

Whose house is that? It's *mine*.

replaces the noun *house*, the object possessed, and shows who possesses it, *me*

IN ENGLISH

Here is a list of the possessive pronouns:

SINGULAR POSSESSOR

1ˢᵀ PERSON		mine
2ᴺᴰ PERSON		yours
3ᴿᴰ PERSON	MASCULINE	his
	FEMININE	hers

PLURAL POSSESSOR

1ˢᵀ PERSON	ours
2ᴺᴰ PERSON	yours
3ᴿᴰ PERSON	theirs

Possessive pronouns only refer to the possessor, not to the object possessed.

My car is red; what color is John's? *His* is blue.

3rd pers. masc. sing.

John's car is blue. What color is yours? *Mine* is white.

1ˢᵗ pers. sing.

Although the object possessed is the same *(car)*, different possessive pronouns *(his* and *mine)* are used because the possessors are different *(John* and *me)*.

Is that John's house? Yes, it is *his*.
Are those John's keys? Yes, they are *his*.

Although the objects possessed are different *(house* and *keys)*, the same possessive pronoun *(his)* is used because the possessor is the same *(John)*.

IN SPANISH

Like English, a Spanish possessive pronoun refers to the possessor. Unlike English, and like all Spanish pronouns, it also agrees in gender and number with the **ANTECEDENT**, that is, with the person or object possessed. In addition, the possessive pronoun is preceded by a definite article that also agrees in gender and number with the antecedent.

Let us look at some English sentences to see how to analyze them in order to find the correct form of the Spanish possessive pronoun.

Where are your books? Mine are in the living room.

1. Find the possessor: *mine* → 1ˢᵗ person singular
2. Find antecedent: *Mine* refers to *books.*
3. Establish the gender and number of the Spanish equivalent of the antecedent.
4. Choose the ending of the possessive pronoun that corresponds in gender and number to step 3 above.
5. Choose the definite article that corresponds in gender and number to step 3 above.

¿Dónde están tus libros? Los míos están en la sala.

1. The 1ˢᵗ person singular possessor *(mine)* is indicated by the first two letters of the 1ˢᵗ person singular possessive pronoun → **mí-**.
2. The antecedent is **libros** *(books).*
3. **Libros** is masculine plural.
4. The masculine plural ending is -**os**.
5. The masculine plural definite article is **los**.

Let us look at the Spanish possessive pronouns to learn how to form them. Each of the possessive pronouns has four forms depending on the gender and number of the antecedent. To choose the proper form follow these steps.

1. Indicate the possessor. This will be shown by the first letters of the possessive pronoun. They are the same initial letters as the stressed possessive adjectives (see *What is a Possessive Adjective?*, p. 100).

SINGULAR POSSESSOR

1ˢᵗ PERSON		mine	**mí-**
2ᴺᴰ PERSON		yours	**tuy-**
3ᴿᴰ PERSON	MASCULINE	his	
	FEMININE	hers yours	**suy-**

PLURAL POSSESSOR

1ˢᵗ PERSON	ours	**nuestr-**
2ᴺᴰ PERSON	yours	**vuestr-**
3ᴿᴰ PERSON	theirs yours	**suy-**

2. Establish the gender and number of the antecedent and choose the definite article and the ending that corresponds to its gender and number.

- antecedent is masculine singular → **el** + first letters of the possessor + **-o**

¿Dónde está **el libro?**	El **mío** está en la mesa.
│	El **tuyo** está en la mesa.
masculine singular	El **suyo** está en la mesa.
	El **nuestro** está en la mesa.
	El **vuestro** está en la mesa.
	El **suyo** está en la mesa.

*Where is **the book?***	*Mine is on the table.*
	Yours is on the table.
	His (hers, yours) is on the table.
	Ours is on the table.
	Yours is on the table.
	Theirs (yours) is on the table.

- antecedent is feminine singular → **la** + first letters of the possessor + **-a**

¿Dónde está **la revista?**	La **mía** está en la mesa.
│	La **tuya** está en la mesa.
feminine singular	La **suya** está en la mesa.
	La **nuestra** está en la mesa.
	La **vuestra** está en la mesa.
	La **suya** está en la mesa.

*Where is **the magazine?***	*Mine is on the table.*
	Yours is on the table.
	His (hers, yours) is on the table.
	Ours is on the table.
	Yours is on the table.
	Theirs (yours) is on the table.

- antecedent is masculine plural → **los** + first letters of the possessor + **-os**

¿Dónde están **los libros?**	Los **míos** están en la mesa.
│	Los **tuyos** están en la mesa.
masculine plural	Los **suyos** están en la mesa.
	Los **nuestros** están en la mesa.
	Los **vuestros** están en la mesa.
	Los **suyos** están en la mesa.

*Where are **the books?***	*Mine are on the table.*
	Yours are on the table.
	His (hers, yours) are on the table.
	Ours are on the table.
	Yours are on the table.
	Theirs (yours) are on the table.

- antecedent is feminine plural → **las** + first letters of the possessor + **-as**

¿Dónde están las revistas? **Las mías** están en la mesa.

feminine plural

Las tuyas están en la mesa.
Las suyas están en la mesa.
Las nuestras están en la mesa.
Las vuestras están en la mesa.
Las suyas están en la mesa.

Where are the magazines? *Mine are on the table.*
Yours are on the table.
His (hers, yours) are on the table.
Ours are on the table.
Yours are on the table.
Theirs (yours) are on the table.

130

3. Select the proper form according to the two steps above.

Let us apply these steps to some examples.

Mary forgot her notebook but we have ours.
  1. POSSESSOR: 1ˢᵗ person plural → **nuestr-**
  2. ANTECEDENT: **cuaderno** *(notebook)* → masculine singular
  3. SELECTION: **el + nuestr- + -o**

María olvidó su cuaderno pero tenemos **el nuestro.**

140

I do not have my books, but John and Mary have theirs.
  1. POSSESSOR: 3ʳᵈ person plural → **suy-**
  2. ANTECEDENT: **libros** *(books)* → masculine plural
  3. SELECTION: **los + suy- + -os**

No tengo mis libros pero Juan y María tienen **los suyos.**

Mary is reading her magazines. John is reading his.
  1. POSSESSOR: 3ʳᵈ person singular → **suy-**
  2. ANTECEDENT: **revistas** *(magazines)* → feminine plural
  3. SELECTION: **las + suy- + -as**

María lee sus revistas. Juan lee **las suyas.**

150

CAREFUL — The definite article is not used when the possessive pronoun follows a form of the verb **ser** *(to be).*

*Is this your coat? No, it's not **mine**. Mine is larger.*
¿Es éste tu abrigo? No, no es **mío.** El **mío** es más grande.

possessive pronoun   article + possessive
without article after **ser**

160

—————————— **SUMMARY** ——————————

Here is a chart you can use as a reference.

SINGULAR POSSESSOR		ANTECEDENT	
		SINGULAR	PLURAL
mine	MASC.	el mío	los míos
	FEM.	la mía	las mías
yours [tú form]	MASC.	el tuyo	los tuyos
	FEM.	la tuya	las tuyas
his, hers, yours [Ud. form]	MASC.	el suyo	los suyos
	FEM.	la suya	las suyas

PLURAL POSSESSOR		ANTECEDENT	
		SINGULAR	PLURAL
ours	MASC.	el nuestro	los nuestros
	FEM.	la nuestra	las nuestras
yours [vosotros form]	MASC.	el vuestro	los vuestros
	FEM.	la vuestra	las vuestras
theirs, yours [Uds. form]	MASC.	el suyo	los suyos
	FEM.	la suya	las suyas

170

— *R E V I E W* —

Underline the possessive pronouns in the sentences below.
- Draw an arrow from the possessive pronoun to its antecedent.
- Circle whether the antecedent is singular (S) or plural (P).
- Using the charts in this section, fill in the Spanish possessive pronoun.

1. I won't take his car. I'll take mine.

   ANTECEDENT IN SPANISH: masculine   S   P

   No tomaré su coche. Tomaré _____

2. I'm not going with my parents. I'm going with hers.

   ANTECEDENT IN SPANISH: masculine   S   P

   No voy con mis padres. Voy con _____

3. These aren't your [tú form] boots. Yours are bigger.

   ANTECEDENT IN SPANISH: feminine   S   P

   No son tus botas. _____ son más grandes.

4. Paul's racquet is broken. He'll use ours.

   ANTECEDENT IN SPANISH: feminine   S   P

   La raqueta de Pablo está rota. Va a usar _____

WHAT IS AN INTERROGATIVE PRONOUN?

An INTERROGATIVE PRONOUN is a word that replaces a noun
and introduces a question. The word *interrogative*
comes from *interrogate,* to question.

> *Who* is coming for dinner?
> |
> refers to a person
>
> *What* did you eat for dinner?
> |
> refers to a thing

In both English and Spanish, a different interrogative
pronoun is used depending on whether it refers to a "person" (human beings and live animals) or a "thing"
(objects and ideas). Also, the form of the interrogative pronoun often changes according to its function in the sentence: subject, direct object, indirect object, and object of a
preposition. We shall look at each type separately.

—INTERROGATIVE PRONOUNS REFERRING TO A PERSON— "WHO, WHOM, WHOSE"

IN ENGLISH

Who is used for the subject of the sentence.

> *Who* lives here?
> |
> subject
>
> *Who* are they?
> |
> subject

Whom is used for the direct object, indirect object, and
object of a preposition.

> *Whom* do you know here?
> |
> direct object
>
> *To whom* did you speak?
> |
> indirect object
>
> *From whom* did you get the book?
> |
> object of preposition *from*

Whose is the possessive form and is used to ask about
possession or ownership.

1

10

20

30

There's a pencil on the floor? *Whose* is it?
|
possessive

They are nice cars. *Whose* are they?
|
possessive

IN SPANISH

The interrogative pronoun referring to persons is always **quién** or **quiénes** regardless of its function within the sentence. The use of **quién** or **quiénes** depends on the number of its ANTECEDENT; i.e., the noun the pronoun refers to.

Who or ***whom*→ quién** or **quiénes**
Since there is no English equivalent for **quiénes**, both the singular and plural forms translate as *who* or *whom* in English.

- a question with **quién** asks for a singular response

    ¿Quién viene? Juan viene.
    | |
    singular subject   singular response

    Who is coming? John is coming.

- a question with **quiénes** asks for a plural response

    ¿Quiénes vienen? Juan, Roberto y Miguel vienen.
    | ‾‾‾‾‾‾‾‾‾‾‾‾‾‾‾‾‾‾‾‾‾
    plural subject   plural response

    Who is coming? John, Robert and Michael are coming.

The two examples below require that you restructure the dangling prepositions (see p. 155).

Who are you leaving with? I'm leaving with Robert. →
With whom are you leaving? I'm leaving with Robert.
| |
singular   singular response

¿Con quién sales? Salgo con Roberto.

Who are you leaving with? I'm leaving with my friends. →
With whom are you leaving? I'm leaving with my friends.
| |
plural   plural response

¿Con quiénes sales? Salgo con mis amigos.

Whose → **de quién** or **de quiénes**
English sentences with *whose* can be re-worded in order to establish the correct word order in Spanish.

1. Replace *whose* with "of whom."

2. Invert the word order of the subject and verb, that is place the verb before the subject.

*Look at the new car. **Whose** is it?*
80
     (word-for-word: *of **whom** is it*)
     Mira el coche nuevo. **¿De quién** es?

───────────────── **DANGLING PREPOSITIONS** ─────────────────
(see *What is a Preposition?*, p. 122)

IN ENGLISH

In English it is difficult to identify the function of pronouns
that are objects of a preposition because the pronouns are
often separated from the preposition of which they are the
object. Consequently, in conversation the interrogative sub-
90
ject pronoun *who* is often used instead of the interrogative
object pronoun *whom*.

     Who did you give the book *to?*
      interrogative   dangling preposition
      pronoun

When a preposition is separated from its object and placed
at the end of a sentence or question, it is called a **DANGLING
PREPOSITION.**

To enable you to establish the function of an interrogative
100
pronoun, you will have to change the structure of the sentence so that the preposition is placed before the interrogative pronoun. In formal English there is a tendency to avoid
dangling prepositions.

    SPOKEN ENGLISH   →   **FORMAL ENGLISH**
    Who did you speak *to?*   *To whom* did you speak?
    instead of *whom* preposition

    Who did you get the book *from?* *From whom* did you get the book?
    instead of *whom*   preposition
110

IN SPANISH

Spanish places prepositions in the same position as formal
English; that is, within the sentence or at the beginning of a
question. By restructuring English sentences or questions
with dangling prepositions you will not only be able to identify the function of interrogative pronouns (and relative pronouns, see p. 167), but also establish the word order for the
Spanish sentence.

Here are a few examples of sentences which have been
restructured to avoid the dangling preposition.
120

Who are you writing to? → *To whom are you writing?*

subject form of   preposition   object form of interr. pronoun
interr. pronoun

¿**A quién** le escribes?

Who are you leaving with? → *With whom are you leaving?*

subject form of   preposition   object form of interr. pronoun
interr. pronoun

¿**Con quién** sales?

130

Who did you buy the gift for? → *For whom did you buy the gift?*

subject form of   preposition   object form of interr. pronoun
interr. pronoun

¿**Para quién** compraste el regalo?

— INTERROGATIVE PRONOUN REFERRING TO A THING — "WHAT"

IN ENGLISH

What refers only to things or ideas. The same form is used for subject, direct object, indirect object, and the object of a preposition.

140

What happened?

subject

What do you want?

direct object

What is the movie about?

object of preposition *about*

IN SPANISH

150

The interrogative pronoun referring to things is always **qué** regardless of its function within the sentence.

What happened?
¿**Qué** pasó?

What do you want?
¿**Qué** quieres?

What is the movie about? → *About what is the movie?*
¿**De qué** trata la película?

−INTERROGATIVE PRONOUNS REQUESTING A SELECTION−
"WHICH ONE, WHICH ONES"

IN ENGLISH

Which (one), which (ones) are used in questions that request the selection of one *(which one,* singular) or more than one *(which ones,* plural) from a group that has already been mentioned. The words *one* and *ones* are often omitted from the phrase. These interrogative pronouns can refer to both persons and things and they do not change according to their function.

All the teachers are here. *Which one* teaches Spanish?
     group   singular subject

I have two cars. *Which one* do you want to take?
     group   singular direct object

The library has many books. *Which ones* do you want?
     group   plural direct object

He has a group of friends. *Which ones* does he live with?
     group   plural object of preposition *with*

IN SPANISH

As in English these interrogative pronouns do not change according to function. Their form does change, however, according to the number of what you want to say: *which one* (singular) → **cuál** or *which ones* (plural) → **cuáles**.

Which one do you need?
¿Cuál necesitas?

Which ones do you need?
¿Cuáles necesitas?

If the English word *one* or *ones* is not expressed, look at the verb. If the verb is singular, use **cuál**; if the verb is plural, use **cuáles**.

Which of the girls is Spanish?
          singular verb
¿Cuál de las chicas **es** española?

Which of the girls are Spanish?
          plural verb
¿Cuáles de las chicas **son** españolas?

CAREFUL — *What is, what are* has two equivalents in Spanish: **qué + ser** or **cuál(-es) + ser.** To determine which to use you need to decide what the expected answer will be.

- expected answer is a definition → **qué + ser**

    What is the Nobel Prize?
    The expected answer is a definition of the Nobel Prize.
    ¿**Qué es** el Premio Nobel?

    What are the Panamerican Games?
    The expected answer is a definition of the
    Panamerican Games.
    ¿**Qué son** los Juegos Panamericanos?

- expected answer provides a number of choices and answers the question *which one(-s)* of many → **cuál(-es) + ser**

    What is your favorite novel?
    The expected answer will explain which novel
    of the many that exist is the favorite.
    ¿**Cuál es** su novela favorita?

    What are the countries of Europe?
    The expected answer will explain which countries
    of the many in the world are European.
    ¿**Cuáles son** los países de Europa?

There is another interrogative pronoun that we will now examine separately since it does not follow the same pattern as above.

──────── **"HOW MUCH, HOW MANY"** ────────

IN ENGLISH

The English interrogative pronouns *how much, how many* are a rare example of English pronouns that change to agree in number with the noun they replace.

    I have money. *How much* do you need?
                  | └──┬──┘
              singular   singular
              noun   pronoun

    I have some stamps. *How many* do you need?
                        | └──┬──┘
                    plural   plural
                    noun   pronoun

IN SPANISH

This interrogative pronoun has four forms that change according to the gender and number of the ANTECEDENT, that is, the noun replaced by the pronoun.

	SINGULAR *how much*	PLURAL *how many*
MASCULINE	cuánto	cuántos
FEMININE	cuánta	cuántas

250

To choose the proper form, follow these steps:

1. Determine the antecedent.
2. Determine the gender of the antecedent.
3. Determine the number of the antecedent.

Let us apply these steps to some examples.

> *I have a lot of paper.* ***How much*** *do you want?*
> 1. ANTECEDENT: **el papel** *(paper)*
> 2. GENDER OF ANTECEDENT: masculine
> 3. NUMBER OF ANTECEDENT: singular
> 4. SELECTION: **cuánto**

260

Tengo mucho papel. ¿Cuánto quieres?

> *I have a lot of soup.* ***How much*** *do you want?*
> 1. ANTECEDENT: **la sopa** *(soup)*
> 2. GENDER OF ANTECEDENT: feminine
> 3. NUMBER OF ANTECEDENT: singular
> 4. SELECTION: **cuánta**

Tengo mucha sopa. ¿Cuánta quieres?

270

> *I have a lot of books.* ***How many*** *do you want?*
> 1. ANTECEDENT: **los libros** *(books)*
> 2. GENDER OF ANTECEDENT: masculine
> 3. NUMBER OF ANTECEDENT: plural
> 4. SELECTION: **cuántos**

Tengo muchos libros. ¿Cuántos quieres?

> *I have a lot of magazines.* ***How many*** *do you want?*
> 1. ANTECEDENT: **las revistas** *(magazines)*
> 2. GENDER OF ANTECEDENT: feminine
> 3. NUMBER OF ANTECEDENT: plural
> 4. SELECTION: **cuántas**

280

Tengo muchas revistas. ¿Cuántas quieres?

— REVIEW —

A. Underline the interrogative pronouns in the questions below.
- Circle the function of the interrogative pronoun in the Spanish sentence: subject (S), object (O), or possessive (P).
- Fill in the Spanish equivalent of the interrogative.

1. *Whose* sweater is this?

    FUNCTION: S   O   P

    RESTRUCTURE THE SENTENCE: _____

    ¿ _____ es este suéter?

2. *Who* are you talking to?

    FUNCTION: S   O   P

    RESTRUCTURE THE SENTENCE: _____

    ¿A _____ le hablas?

3. *Who* is coming to see you? My friends.

    FUNCTION: S   O   P

    ¿ _____ vienen a verte? Mis amigos.

B. Underline the interrogative pronouns in the questions below.
- Circle the function of the interrogative pronouns in English: definition (D) or selection (S).
- Fill in the appropriate Spanish equivalents.

1. What is your favorite movie?

    FUNCTION: D   S

    ¿_____ tu película favorita?

2. What is the White House?

    FUNCTION: D   S

    ¿_____ la Casa Blanca?

3. What are the most popular cars in the world?

    FUNCTION: D   S

    ¿_____ los coches más populares del mundo?

WHAT IS A DEMONSTRATIVE PRONOUN?

A DEMONSTRATIVE PRONOUN is a word that replaces a noun   1
as if pointing to it. The word *demonstrative*
comes from *demonstrate*, to show.

Choose a suit. *This one* is expensive. *That one* is not.

antecedent   points to one suit   points to another suit

In English and Spanish, demonstrative pronouns can be
used in a variety of ways.

───── **"THIS ONE, THAT ONE" AND "THESE, THOSE"** ─────
IN ENGLISH   10
The singular demonstrative pronouns are ***this (one)*** and
that (one); the plural forms are ***these*** and ***those***.

Here are my suitcases. *This one* is big; *those* are small.

antecedent   singular   plural

Choose a book. *Those* are in Spanish; *that one* is in English.

antecedent   plural   singular

This (one), *these* refer to persons or objects near the speaker, and *that (one)*, *those* refer to persons or objects further   20
away from the speaker.

This and *that* are also used to refer to an unspecified
object, idea, or previous statement.

What is *that?*

the object pointed to is unspecified

That is true.

refers to an idea previously expressed

IN SPANISH
Demonstrative pronouns agree in gender with their   30
ANTECEDENT; that is, the noun to which they refer. Their
number depends on whether they refer to one person or
object *(this one, that one)* or to more than one person or
object *(these, those)*. Demonstrative pronouns are the same
words as demonstrative adjectives, except that all pronoun
forms carry a written accent mark in order to distinguish the
pronouns from the adjectives (see pp. 110-12).

As pronouns, these words replace the demonstrative adjective + noun; they agree in number and gender with the noun replaced.

Here is a chart you can use as reference.

To POINT OUT:	SINGULAR		PLURAL	
	MASCULINE	FEMININE	MASCULINE	FEMININE
ITEMS NEAR THE SPEAKER	éste	ésta	éstos	éstas
	this (one)		*these*	
ITEMS NEAR THE THE PERSON SPOKEN TO	ése	ésa	ésos	ésas
	that (one)		*those*	
ITEMS AWAY FROM THE SPEAKER AND PERSON SPOKEN TO	aquél	aquélla	aquéllos	aquéllas
	that one (over there)		*those (over there)*	

To choose the correct form, follow these steps.

1. Find the antecedent.
2. Determine the relationship of the antecedent to the speaker or person spoken to.
3. Determine the gender of the antecedent.
4. Determine the number of the antecedent: *this one, that one* → singular; *these, those* → plural.
5. Based on Steps 2, 3 and 4, choose the correct word from the chart above.

Let us apply these steps to some examples.

Which book do you want? ***This one.***
1. ANTECEDENT: *book* (**libro**)
2. RELATIONSHIP: near the speaker
3. GENDER OF THE ANTECEDENT: **libro** → masculine
4. NUMBER OF THE ANTECEDENT: *this one* → singular
5. SELECTION: **éste**

¿Qué libro quieres? **Éste.**

Which magazine do you want? ***That one.***
1. ANTECEDENT: *magazine* (**revista**)
2. RELATIONSHIP: near the person spoken to
3. GENDER OF THE ANTECEDENT: **revista** → feminine
4. NUMBER OF THE ANTECEDENT: *that one* → singular
5. SELECTION: **ésa**

¿Qué revista quieres? **Ésa.**

*Which notebooks do you want? **Those (over there).***
1. ANTECEDENT: *notebooks* (**cuadernos**)
2. RELATIONSHIP: away from the speaker and the person spoken to
3. GENDER OF THE ANTECEDENT: **cuadernos** → masculine
4. NUMBER OF THE ANTECEDENT: *those* → plural
5. SELECTION: **aquéllos**

¿Qué cuadernos quieres? **Aquéllos.**

*Which suitcases do you want? **These.***
1. ANTECEDENT: *suitcases* (**maletas**)
2. RELATIONSHIP: near the speaker
3. GENDER OF THE ANTECEDENT: **maletas** → feminine
4. NUMBER OF THE ANTECEDENT: *these* → plural
5. SELECTION: **éstas**

¿Qué maletas quieres? **Éstas.**

———— SPANISH NEUTER DEMONSTRATIVE PRONOUNS ————

Spanish also has three demonstrative pronouns that are used to refer to an unspecified object, idea, or previous statement. These pronouns are said to be NEUTER; that is, they have no gender or their gender is not known. These pronouns are INVARIABLE; that is, they do not change form.

esto	*this (one)*
eso	*that (one)*
aquello	*that (one over there)*

Let us look at some examples of these neuter demonstrative pronouns.

*What is **this**?*
Since the antecedent of "this" is unknown, the gender and number of the antecedent is also unknown. The neuter form must be used.

¿Qué es **esto**?

That's not true.
The antecedent of "that" is a previous statement which has no gender. The neuter form must be used.

Eso no es verdad.

*What is **that over there**?*
Since the antecedent of "that over there" is unknown, the gender and number of the antecedent is also unknown. The neuter form must be used.

¿Qué es **aquello**?

There is another demonstrative pronoun which we will now examine separately because it does not follow the same pattern as above.

———————— **"THE ONE, THE ONES"** ————————

IN ENGLISH

The demonstrative pronouns *the one* (singular antecedent) and *the ones* (plural antecedent), followed by the relative pronouns *that, which* or *who,* can begin a relative clause giving us additional information about a person or thing previously mentioned. Since the relative pronouns *that, which* or *who* are often omitted in English, we have indicated them between parentheses (see *What is a Relative Pronoun?,* p. 167).

What book are you reading? I'm reading *the one (that)* you gave me.
>CLAUSE: *the one that you gave me*
>gives us additional information about *the book.*
>NUMBER: *The one* is singular.

Which girls went to Mexico? *The ones who* spoke Spanish.
>CLAUSE: *the ones who spoke Spanish*
>gives us additional information about *the girls.*
>NUMBER: *The ones* is plural.

IN SPANISH

To express *the one (that)* or *the ones (that),* Spanish uses the definite article that agrees with the antecedent **el, la, los,** or **las** followed by the relative pronoun **que.** Unlike English, the relative pronoun must always be stated.

To choose the correct form of *the one (that)* or *the ones (that)* follow these steps.

    1. Find the antecedent.
    2. Determine the gender and number of the antecedent.
    3. Based on step 2 select the appropriate form of the definite article + **que.**

Let us apply these steps to some examples.

>*What book are you reading? The one (that) I bought yesterday.*
>   1. ANTECEDENT: *book* (**libro**)
>   2. GENDER & NUMBER OF THE ANTECEDENT: masculine singular
>   3. SELECTION: **el que**
>¿Qué libro lees? **El que** compré ayer.

>*Which women went to Mexico? The ones who speak Spanish.*
>   1. ANTECEDENT: *women* (**mujeres**)
>   2. GENDER & NUMBER OF THE ANTECEDENT: feminine plural
>   3. SELECTION: **las que**
>¿Qué mujeres fueron a México? **Las que** hablan español.

——————— TO SHOW POSSESSION ———————

IN ENGLISH

You can show possession with an apostrophe after the possessor, without repeating the person or object possessed mentioned in a previous sentence. The person or object possessed is the antecedent.

170

> Do you have a car? No, I use my *father's*.
> | |
>   antecedent   possessor + apostrophe
>
> The word *car* is not repeated after *father*; it is understood.

IN SPANISH

Remember that the apostrophe structure to show possession does not exist in Spanish (see p. 17). For the same reason that "my father's house" can only be expressed with the structure "the house *of* my father," the expression "my father's" can only be expressed with a structure that does not require an apostrophe. This structure corresponds word-for-word to *the one of* (singular antecedent) or *the ones of* (plural antecedent).

180

> Do you have a car? No, I'm using my *father's*.
> | |
>   antecedent   possessor + apostrophe
>   singular   "*the one of* my father"
>
> Do you have your keys? No, I'm using my *father's*.
> | |
>   antecedent   possessor + apostrophe
>   plural   "*the ones of* my father"

190

When the person or object possessed is not stated in the same sentence, Spanish uses the definite article which agrees with the antecedent **el, la, los,** or **las** + **de** *(of)*.

To choose the correct form, follow these steps.

1. Restructure the possessive phrase.
2. Find the antecedent of *the one* or *the ones.*
3. Determine the gender and number of the antecedent.
4. Based on step 3 select the proper form of the definite article + **de.**

200

Let us apply these rules to the following examples.

> *Do you have a car? No, I'm driving my brother's.*
> 1. RESTRUCTURE: My brother's → *the one of* my brother
> 2. ANTECEDENT: *car* (**coche**)
> 3. GENDER & NUMBER OF THE ANTECEDENT: masculine singular
> 4. SELECTION: **el de**
>
> ¿Tienes un coche? No, manejo **el de** mi hermano.

210

Which house are you selling? My mother's.
1. RESTRUCTURE: My mother's → *the one of* my mother
2. ANTECEDENT: *house* (**casa**)
3. GENDER & NUMBER OF THE ANTECEDENT: feminine singular
4. SELECTION: **la de**

¿Qué casa vendes? **La de** mi madre.

Which books are you reading? The teacher's.
1. RESTRUCTURE: The teacher's → *the ones of* the teacher
2. ANTECEDENT: *books* (**libros**)
3. GENDER & NUMBER OF THE ANTECEDENT: masculine plural
4. SELECTION: **los de**

¿Qué libros lees? **Los del** profesor.

— REVIEW —

Circle the demonstrative pronouns in the following sentences.
- Draw an arrow from the demonstrative pronoun to its antecedent.
- Circle if the relationship is near the speaker (NS), near the person spoken to (NPS), or away from both (A).
- Circle if the antecedent is singular (S) or plural (P).
- Fill in the Spanish demonstrative pronoun in the Spanish sentences (see chart p. 162).

1. She did not buy that dress because she wants this one.

RELATIONSHIP TO SPEAKER:	NS	NPS	A
ANTECEDENT IN SPANISH: masculine		S	P

Ella no compró ese vestido porque quiere _____.

2. Which notebook is yours? That one.

RELATIONSHIP TO SPEAKER:	NS	NPS	A
ANTECEDENT IN SPANISH: masculine		S	P

¿Qué cuaderno es tuyo? _____.

3. These new houses are more expensive than those over there.

RELATIONSHIP TO SPEAKER:	NS	NPS	A
ANTECEDENT IN SPANISH: feminine		S	P

Estas casas nuevas son más caras que _____.

WHAT IS A RELATIVE PRONOUN?

A **RELATIVE PRONOUN** is a word used at the beginning of a clause giving additional information about someone or something previously mentioned.

1

clause
additional information about <i>the book</i>

I'm reading the book *that* the teacher recommended.

A relative pronoun serves two purposes:

1. As a pronoun it stands for a noun previously mentioned. The noun to which it refers is called the **ANTECEDENT**.

10

This is the boy <i>who</i> broke the window.

antecedent of the relative pronoun <i>who</i>

2. It introduces a **SUBORDINATE CLAUSE**; that is, a group of words having a subject and a verb which cannot stand alone because it does not express a complete thought. A subordinate clause is dependent on a **MAIN CLAUSE**; that is, another group of words having a subject and a verb which can stand alone as a complete sentence.

20

main clause   subordinate clause

Here comes the boy <i>who broke the window.</i>

verb   subject subject verb

A subordinate clause that starts with a relative pronoun is also called a **RELATIVE CLAUSE**. In the example above, the relative clause starts with the relative pronoun *who* and gives us additional information about the antecedent *boy*.

Relative clauses are very common. We use them in everyday speech without giving much thought as to why and how we construct them. The relative pronoun allows us to combine two thoughts which have a common element into a single sentence.

30

    SENTENCE A I met the teacher.

    SENTENCE B He teaches Spanish.

    COMBINED I met the teacher *who* teaches Spanish.

When sentences are combined with a relative pronoun, the relative pronoun can have different functions in the relative clause. It can be the subject, the direct object, the indirect object or the object of a preposition.

The selection of a relative pronoun often depends not only on its function in the relative clause, but also on whether its antecedent is a "person" (human beings and animals) or a "thing" (objects and ideas).

IN ENGLISH ————————————————————————

In an English sentence, relative pronouns can sometimes be omitted.

> The book *that* I'm reading is interesting.
> |
>   relative pronoun

> The book I'm reading is interesting.
> |
>   relative pronoun omitted

IN SPANISH ————————————————————————

The main difference between Spanish and English relative pronouns is that relative pronouns must always be expressed in Spanish sentences.[1]

Since the selection of a relative pronoun depends on its function in the relative clause, we shall look at each function separately.

—————— **SUBJECT OF THE RELATIVE CLAUSE** ——————
(see *What is a Subject?*, p. 23)

IN ENGLISH

There are three relative pronouns that can be used as subjects of a relative clause, depending on whether the relative pronoun refers to a person or a thing. When it is the subject of a relative clause, a relative pronoun is never omitted.

1. PERSON — *Who* or *that* is used as subject of the relative clause.

> She is the only student *who* answered all the time.
> She is the only student *that* answered all the time.
> | |
>   antecedent   relative pronoun
>   subject of *answered*

---

[1]This handbook will not deal with the forms of **el que, el cual,** or **cuyo** since they are not included in most beginning textbooks.

2. THING — *Which* or *that* is used as subject of the relative clause.

> The movie *which* is so popular was filmed in Spain.
> The movie *that* is so popular was filmed in Spain.
> | |
> antecedent relative pronoun
>   subject of *is*

Notice that the relative pronoun subject is always followed by a verb.

IN SPANISH

There is only one relative pronoun that can be used as subject of a relative clause.

1. & 2. PERSON OR THING — **Que** is used as the subject of a relative clause.

> *John is the student **who** answered.*
> Juan es el estudiante **que** respondió.

> *This is the phone **which (that)** isn't working.*
> Aquí está el teléfono **que** no funciona.

——— COMBINING SENTENCES: RELATIVE PRONOUN SUBJECT ———

IN ENGLISH

> SENTENCE A The students passed the exam.
> SENTENCE B They studied.

1. Identify the element the two sentences have in common.
> Both *the students* and *they* refer to the same persons.

2. The common element in the first sentence is called the **ANTECEDENT** of the relative pronoun; that is, the person or thing to which the relative pronoun refers. The relative pronoun always replaces the common element in the second sentence.
> *The students* is the antecedent.
> *They* will be replaced by a relative pronoun.

3. The relative pronoun in the relative clause has the same function as the word it replaces.
> *They* is the subject of *studied*. Therefore,
> the relative pronoun will be the subject of *studied*.

4. Choose the relative pronoun according to whether its antecedent is a person or a thing.
> *They* refers to *students*. Therefore, its antecedent
> is a person.

5. Select the relative pronoun.

> *Who* or *that* is the subject relative pronoun
> referring to a person.

6. Place the relative pronoun at the beginning of the second sentence, thus forming a relative clause.

> *who* studied
> *that* studied

7. Place the relative clause right after its antecedent.

> *The students **who** studied passed the exam.*
> *The students **that** studied passed the exam.*
>   antecedent relative clause

IN SPANISH

> SENTENCE A   Los estudiantes aprobaron el examen.
> SENTENCE B   Estudiaron.

Follow the same steps as under In English above, skipping step 4.

> Los estudiantes **que** estudiaron aprobaron el examen.
>   antecedent   relative clause

——— DIRECT OBJECT OF THE RELATIVE CLAUSE ———

(see pp. 124-5 in *What are Direct and Indirect Objects?*)

IN ENGLISH

There are three relative pronouns that can be used as direct objects of a relative clause, depending on whether the relative pronoun refers to a person or a thing. When it is the direct object of a relative clause, a relative pronoun is often omitted.

1. PERSON — **Whom** or **that** is used as direct object of a relative clause.

> This is the student *(whom)* I saw yesterday.
> This is the student *(that)* I saw yesterday.
>   antecedent   direct object of *saw*

2. THING — **Which** or **that** is used as direct object of a relative clause.

> This is the book *(which)* Paul bought.
> This is the book *(that)* Paul bought.
>   antecedent direct object of *bought*

Notice that when expressed the relative pronoun direct object is always followed by a noun or pronoun.

IN SPANISH

There is only one relative pronoun that can be used as direct object of a relative clause. Unlike English the relative pronoun is never omitted.

1. & 2. PERSON OR THING — **Que** is used as direct object of a relative clause.

We have included the relative pronouns in the English sentences below to show you what the Spanish relative pronoun relates to; however, since relative pronouns are often omitted in English, we have put them between parentheses.

*This is the student **(whom)** John saw last night.*
Este es el estudiante **que** Juan vio anoche.

*This is the book **(that)** John bought.*
Este es el libro **que** Juan compró.

— **COMBINING SENTENCES: RELATIVE PRONOUN DIRECT OBJECT** —

IN ENGLISH

SENTENCE A   The Spanish teacher is nice.
SENTENCE B   I met her today.

1. COMMON ELEMENT: *Spanish teacher* and *her*
2. ELEMENT TO BE REPLACED: *her*
3. FUNCTION OF *HER*: direct object
4. ANTECEDENT: *the Spanish teacher* is a person.
5. SELECTION: *whom* or *that*
6. RELATIVE CLAUSE: *whom (that)* I met today
7. PLACEMENT: antecedent *(the Spanish teacher)* + relative clause

*The Spanish teacher **(whom)** I met today is nice.*
*The Spanish teacher **(that)** I met today is nice.*
      | ⌐———————¬
  antecedent   relative clause

When the relative pronoun *whom* or *that* is left out ("The Spanish teacher I met today is nice"), it is difficult to identify the two clauses.

IN SPANISH

SENTENCE A   La profesora de español es simpática.
SENTENCE B   La conocí hoy.

Follow the same steps as under In English above, skipping step 4.

La profesora de español **que** conocí hoy es simpática.
    | ⌐————————¬
  antecedent   relative clause

— INDIRECT OBJECT AND OBJECT OF A PREPOSITION — IN A RELATIVE CLAUSE

(see pp. 125-8 in *What are Direct and Indirect Objects?*)

Both the relative pronoun as an indirect object and the relative pronoun as an object of a preposition involve prepositions.

Mary is the person to *whom* he gave the present.

relative pronoun indirect object (object of preposition *to*)

Mary is the person with *whom* he went out.

relative pronoun object of the preposition *with*

IN ENGLISH

It is difficult to identify the function of these relative pronouns in English because they are often separated from the preposition of which they are the object. When a preposition is separated from its object and placed at the end of a sentence it is called a DANGLING PREPOSITION (see p. 155).

Mary is the person *that* he went out *with*.

relative pronoun   dangling preposition

There are two relative pronouns used as indirect objects or as objects of a preposition in a relative clause, depending on whether the relative pronoun refers to a person or a thing. When it is the indirect object or the object of a preposition in a relative clause, a relative pronoun is often omitted.

1. PERSON — *Whom* is used as indirect object and as object of a preposition.

Here is the student to *whom* I was speaking.

antecedent   indirect object (object of preposition *to*)

Here is the student about *whom* I was speaking.

antecedent   object of preposition *about*

The above sentences are usually expressed as follows:

Here is the student I was speaking *to*.
Here is the student I was speaking *about*.

These sentences without a relative pronoun and with a dangling preposition have to be restructured in order to establish the function of the relative pronoun in the Spanish sentences. To restructure the English sentences, follow these steps.

1. Identify the antecedent.
2. Place the preposition after the antecedent.   250
3. Add the relative pronoun *whom* after the preposition.

SPOKEN ENGLISH →	RESTRUCTURED
Here is the student	Here is the student
I was speaking *to*.	*to whom* I was speaking.

indirect object (object of preposition *to*)

Here is the student	Here is the student
I was speaking *about*.	*about whom* I was speaking.

object of preposition *about*

    260

2. THING — **Which** is used as indirect object and as object of a preposition.

Here is the museum he gave the painting *to*.

antecedent   dangling preposition

SPOKEN ENGLISH →	RESTRUCTURED
Here is the museum	Here is the museum
he gave the painting *to*.	*to which* he gave the painting.

indirect object (object of preposition *to*)

    270

IN SPANISH

The choice of the relative pronoun used as an indirect object or as an object of a preposition depends on whether the relative pronoun refers to a person or a thing. Unlike English, the relative pronoun is never omitted.

1. PERSON — **Quien** or **quienes** is used as the indirect object and as object of a preposition of a relative clause. You will often need to restructure the English sentence before attempting to put it into Spanish.

    280

SPOKEN ENGLISH →	RESTRUCTURED
John is the boy	*John is the boy*
I'm going with.	*with whom I'm going*.

preposition   object of preposition *with*

Juan es el chico con **quien** salgo.

SPOKEN ENGLISH →	RESTRUCTURED
The girls I'm writing	*The girls*
to live in Madrid.	*to whom I'm writing live in*
	Madrid.

preposition   object of preposition *to*

    290

Las chicas **a quienes** les escribo viven en Madrid.

2. THING — In conversational Spanish a preposition + **que** is generally used.

SPOKEN ENGLISH   →   RESTRUCTURED
This is the book   *This is the book*
*I was talking **about**.*   ***about** which I was talking.*
　　　　　|　　　　　　　　　|
　preposition　object of preposition *about*

Este es el libro **de que** hablaba.

300
─────────────────── **SUMMARY** ───────────────────

Here is a chart you can use as reference:

FUNCTION IN RELATIVE CLAUSE:	ANTECEDENT	
	PERSON	THING
SUBJECT	*who, that* que	*that, which* que
DIRECT OBJECT	*whom, that* que	*that, which* que
INDIRECT OBJECT OBJECT OF PREPOSITION	*whom, that* quien(-es)	*that, which* que

As you can see, Spanish relative pronouns are relatively easy: basically **que** is used in all cases and for all functions, except indirect objects and objects of a preposition referring to persons when Spanish uses **quien** or **quienes**. The difficulty arises from the English usage of relative pronouns. Your ability to handle Spanish relative pronouns correctly will depend on two factors: 1. reinstating relative pronouns which are often omitted in English and 2. restructuring English dangling prepositions.

To find the appropriate Spanish relative pronoun you must go through the following steps.

1. Find the relative clause.
   ▪ restructure the English clause if there is a dangling preposition
   ▪ add the relative pronoun if it has been omitted

2. Establish the function of the relative pronoun in the Spanish sentence:

SUBJECT — If the relative pronoun is the subject of the English sentence, it will be the subject of the Spanish sentence → **que**.

DIRECT OBJECT — If the Spanish verb takes a direct object → **que.**

INDIRECT OBJECT OR OBJECT OF A PREPOSITION — Establish whether the relative pronoun refers to a person or a thing.

- a person → preposition + **quien** (sing.) or preposition + **quienes** (pl.)
- a thing → preposition + **que**

3. Based on step 2 select the Spanish form (see p. 174).

4. Place the relative pronoun and its clause right after the antecedent.

Let's apply the steps outlined above to the following sentences:

> *The lady* ***who*** *is my neighbor is from Colombia.*
> 1. RELATIVE CLAUSE: who is my neighbor
> 2. ANTECEDENT: *lady* **(señora)**
> 3. FUNCTION OF RELATIVE PRONOUN IN SPANISH: subject of relative clause
> 4. SELECTION: **que**
> 5. PLACEMENT: antecedent *(señora)* + **que** + clause

La señora **que** es mi vecina es de Colombia.

> *Here are the books* ***(that)*** *I bought yesterday.*
> 1. RELATIVE CLAUSE: that I bought yesterday
> 2. ANTECEDENT: *books* **(libros)**
> 3. FUNCTION OF RELATIVE PRONOUN IN SPANISH: direct object of **comprar** *(to buy)*
> 4. SELECTION: **que**
> 5. PLACEMENT: antecedent *(libros)* + **que** + clause

Aquí están los libros **que** compré ayer.

> *Peter and Joe are the boys I was talking to.* →
> RESTRUCTURE: *Peter and Joe are the boys* ***to whom*** *I was talking.*
> 1. RELATIVE CLAUSE: to whom I was talking
> 2. ANTECEDENT: *boys* **(chicos)**
> 3. FUNCTION OF RELATIVE PRONOUN IN SPANISH: object of preposition *to*
> 4. SELECTION: **quienes**
> 5. PLACEMENT: antecedent *(chicos)* + **a quienes** + clause

Pedro y José son los chicos **a quienes** hablaba.

Relative pronouns can be tricky to handle and this handbook provides only a simple outline. Refer to your Spanish textbook for additional rules.

—— RELATIVE PRONOUNS WITHOUT ANTECEDENTS ——

There are relative pronouns that do not refer to a specific noun or pronoun. Instead, they refer to an antecedent which has not been expressed or to an entire idea.

340

350

360

370

IN ENGLISH

There are two relative pronouns that can be used without an antecedent: *what* and *which.*

What — does not refer to a specific noun or pronoun.[1]

> I don't know *what* happened.
> |
> no antecedent
> subject

> Here is *what* I read.
> |
> no antecedent
> direct object

Which — refers to an entire idea, not to a specific noun or pronoun.

> She didn't do well, *which* is too bad.
> |
> antecedent: the fact that she didn't do well
> subject of *is*

> You speak many languages, *which* I envy.
> |
> antecedent: the fact that you speak many languages
> direct object of *envy (I* is the subject)

IN SPANISH

When a relative pronoun does not have a specific antecedent, the pronoun **lo que** is used. It is used in conversational Spanish and refers to an idea or previously mentioned statement or concept that has no gender. It can function as a subject or object.

Here are a few examples.

> *What bothers me most is the heat.*
> 1. RELATIVE CLAUSE: what bothers me most
> 2. ANTECEDENT: none expressed in the sentence
> 3. FUNCTION OF RELATIVE PRONOUN IN SPANISH: subject of relative clause
> 4. SELECTION: **lo que**
>
> Lo que me molesta más es el calor.

> *What you are saying isn't true.*
> 1. RELATIVE CLAUSE: what you are saying
> 2. ANTECEDENT: none expressed in the sentence

---

[1]The relative pronoun *what* (meaning *that which*) should not be confused with other uses of *what;* as an interrogative pronoun *(What do you want? ¿Qué quieres?,* see p. 156), and as an interrogative adjective *(What book do you want? ¿Qué libro quieres?,* see p. 107).

3. FUNCTION OF RELATIVE PRONOUN IN SPANISH: direct object of **decir**
   (to say)
4. SELECTION: **lo que**

Lo que dices no es verdad.

420

*He doesn't speak Spanish, **which** will be a problem.*
   1. RELATIVE CLAUSE: which will be a problem
   2. ANTECEDENT: entire previous clause: "he doesn't speak Spanish"
   3. FUNCTION OF RELATIVE PRONOUN IN SPANISH: subject of relative
      clause
   4. SELECTION: **lo que**

No habla español **lo que** será un problema.

— REVIEW —

Underline the relative pronoun in the sentences below.
- Circle the antecedent or (NA) if there is no antecedent.
- Circle the function of the relative pronoun: subject (S), direct
  object (DO), indirect object (IO), object of a preposition (OP),
  or possessive (P).
- Using the chart on p. 174, fill in the Spanish relative pronoun
  in the Spanish sentences below.

1. I received the letter that you sent me. NA
   *(to send → **enviar**)*

   FUNCTION IN SPANISH: S   DO   IO   OP   P

   Recibí la carta _____ me enviaste.

2. That is the woman who speaks Spanish. NA

   FUNCTION IN SPANISH: S   DO   IO   OP   P

   Esa es la mujer _____ habla español.

3. Paul is the student I traveled with. NA

   RESTRUCTURE:

   _____

   FUNCTION IN SPANISH: S   DO   IO   OP   P

   Pablo es el estudiante con _____ viajé.

4. What he said was a lie. NA

   FUNCTION IN SPANISH: S   DO   IO   OP   P

   _____ dijo fue una mentira.

CHAPTER

45

WHAT ARE INDEFINITES AND NEGATIVES?

Words that refer to persons, things, or periods of time that
are not specific or that are not clearly
defined are called INDEFINITES.

I saw *someone* in the kitchen.

not a specific person → indefinite word

Words that deny the existence of persons, things, or periods
of time or that contradict ideas or
previous statements are called NEGATIVES.

I *never* met her mother.

not a period of time → negative word

IN ENGLISH

Some common indefinites are *someone, anybody, something, someday.* These indefinite words are often paired
with negative words which are opposite in meaning: *no
one, nobody, nothing,* and *never.*

INDEFINITES	NEGATIVES
someone anyone	*no one*
somebody anybody	*nobody*
something anything	*nothing*
someday any day	*never*

In conversation indefinites frequently appear in questions
while negatives appear in answers.

QUESTION:	Is *anyone* coming tonight?
ANSWER:	*No one.*
QUESTION:	Do you have *anything* for me?
ANSWER:	*Nothing.*
QUESTION:	Are you going to Europe *someday*?
ANSWER:	*Never.*

English sentences can be made negative in one of two ways.

- the word *not* appears before the main verb (see *What are Affirmative and Negative Sentences?*, p. 45)

40

> I am studying.
> I am *not* studying.

- a negative word can be used in any part of the sentence

> *No one* is coming.
> He has *never* seen a movie.

English allows only one negative word (either *not* or any of the other negative words) in a sentence. When a sentence contains the word *not,* another negative word cannot be used in that sentence. (See chart p. 178.)

50

> "I am *not* studying *nothing*" [incorrect English]
> | |
>   *not*   negative word
> This sentence contains a double negative: *not* and *nothing*.

When a sentence contains the word *not,* the indefinite word that is the opposite of the negative word must be used (see chart p. 178).

> I am *not* studying *anything*.
> |
> indefinite word opposite of negative word *nothing*

60

Let us look at another example.

> I have said *nothing* to them.
> |
>   negative word
> *Nothing* is the one negative word.

> I have *not* said *anything* to them.
> |
>   indefinite word
> This sentence contains *not*; therefore, the word *anything*
> is substituted for *nothing*.

70

> "I have *not* said *nothing*" [incorrect English]
> This sentence contains a double negative: *not* and *nothing*.

IN SPANISH

As in English, the indefinite and negative words exist as pairs of opposites. Here is a chart of the most common indefinites and negatives.

INDEFINITES		NEGATIVES	
something	**algo**	**nada**	*nothing*
some, any	**algún** **alguno**	**ningún** **ninguno**	*none*
someone *somebody*	**alguien**	**nadie**	*no one* *nobody*
someday *always* *sometimes*	**algún día** **siempre** **a veces**	**nunca**	*never*
also, too	**también**	**tampoco**	*not...either*
either, or	**o**	**ni**	*neither...nor*

Notice that most indefinites begin with the letters **alg-** and the negatives begin with **n-**.

Contrary to English, a negative word, not an indefinite, is used in a Spanish sentence that contains **no** meaning *not*. An indefinite word cannot appear in a negative Spanish sentence.

> **No** tengo **nada.**
> not + negative word *(nothing)*
>
> *I do **not** have **anything.***
> not + indefinite word *(anything)*

The following formula for indefinites and negatives in English and Spanish will help you use them correctly.

> ENGLISH →   *not* + main verb + indefinite word(s)
> SPANISH →   **no** + verb + negative word(s)

As you can see from the example above, Spanish requires that you use a construction that would be incorrect in English, i.e., two negatives in the same sentence.

> **No** veo a **nadie.**
> **no** + negative word
> [word-for-word: *I do not see nobody*]
>
> *I do **not** see **anybody.***
> not + indefinite word

Follow these steps to find the Spanish equivalent of an English sentence with *not* + an indefinite word:

1. Locate the indefinite word in the English sentence.

2. From the chart on p. 178 choose the negative word that is the opposite of the English indefinite word.

3. Restructure the English sentence using *not* + the negative word chosen under 2 above.

4. Put the sentence into Spanish.

Let us apply the steps above to the following sentences.   130

> *I do not want to eat anything.*
> 1. IDENTIFY THE INDEFINITE: anything
> 2. SELECT THE NEGATIVE: nothing
> 3. RESTRUCTURE: "I do *not* want to eat *nothing*"

No quiero comer **nada.**

> *I don't (not) know anyone here.*
> 1. IDENTIFY THE INDEFINITE: anyone
> 2. SELECT THE NEGATIVE: no one
> 3. RESTRUCTURE: "I do*n't* know *no one* here"   140

No conozco a **nadie** aquí.

— *REVIEW* —

Underline the indefinite word or phrase in the following sentences.
- Select the negative word that is the opposite of the English indefinite word.
- Restructure the English sentence using *not* + the negative word chosen above.
- Fill in the negative phrase in the Spanish sentence.

1. I'm not going to do that ever.

    NEGATIVE WORD/PHRASE:_____

    RESTRUCTURE:_____

    No voy a hacer eso _____.

2. John isn't going to the party either.

    NEGATIVE WORD/PHRASE:_____

    RESTRUCTURE:_____

    Juan no va a la fiesta _____.

3. We don't have anything to do.

    NEGATIVE WORD/PHRASE:_____

    RESTRUCTURE:_____

    No tenemos _____ que hacer.

4. They don't know anyone in Bogotá.

    NEGATIVE WORD/PHRASE:_____

    RESTRUCTURE:_____

    No conocen a _____ en Bogotá.

1. What is a Noun? 1. students, classroom, teacher 2. Wilsons, tour, Mexico 3. figure skating, event, Winter Olympics 4. Buenos Aires, capital, Argentina, city 5. truth, fiction 6. boss, intelligence, sense, humor

2. What is Meant by Gender? 1. M 2. ? 3. F 4. ? 5. ? 6. F 7. ?

3. What is Meant by Number? 1. P 2. S 3. S 4. P 5. P 6. S

4. What are Articles? 1. los 2. una 3. unas 4. el 5. un 6. las 7. unos 8. una 9. la

5. What is the Possessive? 1. the parents of some children 2. the office of the doctor 3. the speed of a car 4. the soccer coach of the girls 5. the mother of Gloria Smith

6. What is a Verb? 1. purchase 2. were 3. enjoyed, preferred 4. ate, finished, went 5. was, to see, struggle, to get 6. attended, to celebrate

7. What is the Infinitive? 1. to do 2. study 3. to learn 4. leave 5. to travel

8. What is a Subject? 1. Q: What rang? A: The bell. (S) Q: Who ran out? A: The children. (P) 2. Q: Who took the order? A: One waiter. (S) Q: Who brought the food? A: Another. (S) 3. Q: Who voted? A: The first-year students (or The students) (P) 4. Q: Who says? A: They. (P) Q: What is a beautiful language? A: Spanish. (S)

9. What is a Pronoun? The antecedent is between parentheses. 1. she (Mary); him (Peter) 2. they (coat, dress) 3. herself (Isabel) 4. we (Robert, I) 5. it (book)

10. What is a Subject Pronoun? A. 1. 1ˢᵗ person, singular → yo 2. 3ʳᵈ person, singular → 0 3. 1ˢᵗ person, plural → nosotros *or* nosotras 4. 3ʳᵈ person, plural → 0 5. 3ʳᵈ person, plural → ellos 6. 3ʳᵈ person, plural → ellas B. 1. ustedes/ustedes 2. tú/tú 3. usted/usted 4. vosotros/ustedes 5. tú/tú 6. usted/usted

11. What is a Verb Conjugation? STEM: compr- CONJUGATION: yo compro; tú compras; él/ella/Ud. compra; nosotros compramos; vosotros compráis; ellos/ellas/Uds. compran

12. What are Auxiliary Verbs? English auxiliaries not used as auxiliaries in Spanish are in *italics*. 1. *will* 2. "are" is a Spanish auxiliary and is expressed with **estar** 3. *did* 4. "had" is a Spanish auxiliary and is expressed with **haber** 5. *do*

13. What are Affirmative and Negative Sentences? Words that indicate the negative are in *italics*. These italicized words are the same words that would not appear in the Spanish negative sentence. 1. We *do not (don't)* want to leave class early. 2. He *did*

not (didn't) do his homework yesterday. 3. Teresa *will not (won't)* go to Chile this summer. 4. Robert *cannot (can't)* go to the restaurant with us.

14. What are Declarative and Interrogative Sentences? Words that indicate the interrogative are in *italics*. These italicized words are the same words that would not appear in the Spanish negative sentence. A. 1. *Did* Richard and Kathy study all evening? 2. *Does* your brother eat a lot? 3. *Do* the girl's parents speak Spanish? B. 1. My mother and father went to the movies, didn't they?

15. What are Some Equivalents of "to be"? A. 1. CR → ser 2. CN → estar 3. CN → estar 4. CR → ser 5. CN → estar 6. CN → estar 7. CR → ser B. 1. L → estar 2. P → hay 3. L → estar 4. P → hay

17. What is the Present Tense? 1. reads 2. is reading → lee 3. does read → lee 4. is reading → lee

18. What is the Past Tense? IMPERFECT: was, was checking, was handling, was crying, was, was leaving PRETERITE: went, arrived, ran, dropped, tried, ducked, grabbed, brought, comforted, smiled, got

19. What is a Participle? 1. P 2. PP 3. PP 4. P

20. What are the Continuous Tenses? 1. P 2. PT 3. PT 4. P 5. P

22. What is the Subjunctive? 1. S 2. S 3. I 4. S 5. S 6. S 7. I

23. What is the Imperative? A. 1. Study for the exam. 2. Let's go to the movies every weekend. 3. Eat more fruit and vegetables. B. 1. Don't sleep in class. 2. Don't work so much. 3. Let's not eat out tonight.

24. What are the Perfect Tenses? 1. had gone, PP 2. has left, P 3. shall have graduated, FP 4. would have studied, CP; had remembered, PP 5. have seen, P

25. What is the Future Tense? 1. will study, study 2. 'll (shall) clean, clean 3. shall leave, leave 4. won't (will not) finish, finish 5. will be, be

26. What is the Conditional? 1. P, F 2. C, IS 3. C or IS 4. P, F 5. PT, C 6. PS, CP

27. What is Meant by Active and Passive Voice? 1. cow, Ac, PP 2. Bob's parents, Pa, PP 3. bank, Ac, P 4. everyone, Ac, F 5. all, Pa, F

29. What is a Descriptive Adjective? The noun or pronoun described is between parentheses. 1. young (man), Spanish (newspaper) 2. pretty (she), new (dress), red (dress) 3. interesting (it) 4. old (piano), good (music) 5. tired (Paul), long (walk)

30. What is a Possessive Adjective? The noun possessed is between parentheses. 1. my (book), S → mi 2. your (boots), P → tus 3. his (mother), S → su 4. our (children), P → nuestros

31. What is an Interrogative Adjective? A. The noun modified is between parentheses. 1. which (book) 2. what (exercises) 3. which (house) B. The noun modified is between parentheses. 1. how many (shirts), P → Cuántas 2. how much (wine), S → Cuánto 3. how many (telephones), P → Cuántos 4. how much (salad), S → Cuánta

32. What is a Demonstrative Adjective? The noun modified is between parentheses. 1. that (restaurant), S → ese 2. those (houses), P → Aquellas 3. these (shoes), P → estos 4. this (magazine), S → esta

33. What is Meant by Comparison of Adjectives? The noun modified is between parentheses. 1. older (teacher), C+ 2. less intelligent (he), C- 3. as tall as (Mary), C= 4. the worst (boy), S 5. better (student), C+

34. What is an Adverb? The word modified is between parentheses. 1. early (arrived) 2. really (quickly), quickly (learned) 3. too (tired) 4. reasonably (secure) 5. very (well), well (speaks)

35. What is a Conjunction? The words to be circled are in *italics*; the words to be underlined are plain. 1. Mary *and* Paul; French *or* Spanish 2. She did not study *because* she was too tired. 3. Not only had he forgotten his ticket, *but* he had forgotten his passport as well.

36. What is a Preposition? 1. toward, of 2. from 3. around 4. at 5. between

37. What are Objects? 1. Q: The children took what? A: A shower → DO 2. Q: They ate what? A: The meal → DO Q: They ate with whom? A: With their friends → OP 3. Q: He sent what? A: A present → DO Q: He sent a present to whom? A: To his brother → IO

38. What is an Object Pronoun? The words to be underlined are in parentheses. 1. (it) DO, DO, book, S → lo 2. (them) DO, DO, magazines, P → las 3. (them) IO, IO, P → les 4. (him) IO, IO, S, M → le

39. What are Object of Preposition Pronouns? 1. them, P, F → ellas 2. her, S, F → ella 3. you, S, NA → ti 4. us, P, NA → nosotros or nosotras

40. What are Reflexive Pronouns and Verbs? A. 1. herself → se 2. yourself → te 3. ourselves → nos 4. themselves → se B. 1. each other, Rp 2. themselves, Rx 3. each other, Rp 4. myself, Rx 5. each other Rp

41. What is a Possessive Pronoun? The antecedent is between parentheses. 1. mine (car), S → el mío 2. hers (parents), P → los suyos 3. yours (boots), P → Las tuyas 4. ours (racket), S → la nuestra

42. What is an Interrogative Pronoun? A. The words to be underlined are in parentheses. 1. (Whose) P, Of whom is the sweater → De quién 2. (who), O, To whom are you talking → quién 3. (who), S → Quiénes B. The words to be underlined are between parentheses. 1. (What), S → Cuál 2. (What), D → Qué 3. (What), S → Cuáles

43. What is a Demonstrative Pronoun? The antecedent is between parentheses. 1. this one (dress), NS, S → éste 2. that one (notebook), NPS, S → Ése 3. those over there (houses), A, P → aquéllas

44. What is a Relative Pronoun? The words to be circled are between parentheses. 1. that (letter), DO → que 2. who (woman), S → que 3. Paul is the student with whom I traveled. whom (student), OP → quien 4. what (no antecedent), S → lo que

45. What are Indefinites and Negatives? The words to be underlined are between parentheses. 1. (ever) never; I'm not going to do that never → nunca 2. (either) neither; John isn't going to the party neither → tampoco 3. (anything), nothing; we don't have nothing to do → nada 4. (anyone), no one; they don't know no one in Bogotá → nadie